Unskilled Labourer and World Statesman

A portrait of Ernest Bevin
1881-1951

THE UN

KEELE

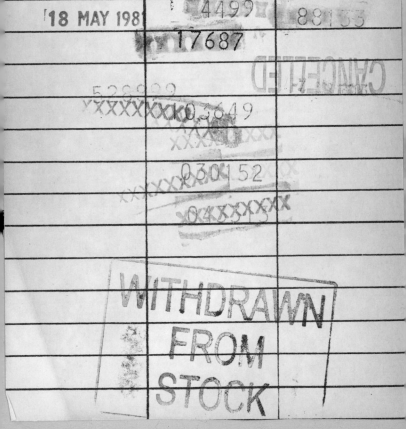

Mark Stephens

Ernest Bevin - Unskilled Labourer and World Statesman 1881-1951

A TGWU Publication

Published by the Transport & General Workers Union 1981

ISBN 0–907475–00–0

Printed in Great Britain by
Richard Clay (The Chaucer Press) Ltd,
Bungay, Suffolk.

TGWU
Transport House,
Smith Square,
London SW1P 3JB

Contents

Acknowledgements

In writing this book I have received great encouragement and help from a large number of people. It is not possible to list all of them by name but I would especially like to mention: Mr Stephen Attmore, Mr Peter Batty, Lord Bullock, Mr Moss Evans, Miss Julia Harrison of Harlow Library, Sir John Hunter, Mr Jack Jones, Mr Arthur Marsh, Mr Larry Smith, Mr Regan Scott, Sir David Stephens, Sir Mark Turner, Miss Pat White of Deborah Rogers Ltd, Mr George Wright, Mr and Mrs Sydney Wynne, and Mr Robert Yeatman.

In expressing my appreciation for all the help I have received I do not wish to involve anyone in responsibility for what I have written. This remains mine alone.

The author and publisher wish to thank the following for permission to quote copyright material: William Heinemann Ltd for *The Life and Times of Ernest Bevin* by Alan Bullock and Hutchinsons Publishing Group for *Ernest Bevin* by Francis Williams.

For Photos: TGWU archive, Labour Party Library, Keystone, Press Association, BBC Hulton, Sport and General and *The Sun*.

'Ill fares the land, to hastening ills a prey,
Where wealth accumulates, and men decay' –
From *Sweet Auburn* by Oliver Goldsmith
and often quoted by Ernest Bevin.

Foreword

Ernest Bevin both developed, and exercised power on behalf of ordinary working people for a long time. He was a Cabinet Minister for a decade of historic importance to the nation, and indeed, the world. And he was undoubtedly the best known trade union figure of the first half of this century.

Inevitably much that he did in those years during the building of the TGWU and developing the broader labour movement and at the same time exercising political influence, was controversial. The closer to power anyone is, it seems, the more likely there will be controversy about their views and decisions, and I am sure Bevin would have welcomed a re-appraisal of his achievements in this spirit.

As my colleague Len Murray said at last year's Bevin Memorial Lecture, Bevin's times are not our times. Those years are receding very rapidly now, but, frankly, their echoes have been loud in the past year or so, and this plain-told story of Bevin's life and times will help to remind us all of what differences divide us from those years, where progress has been made, and where injustice still remains unchecked.

In addition to this broader purpose, there are two related reasons for a revival of interest in Bevin's life, aside from the natural wish of his union to celebrate the birth centenary of its founder general secretary.

Firstly, it is arguable that the proper role of trades unions is now as fiercely contested on the political stage – though it is rarely off stage, in truth – as it has been since the time of the General Strike, while mass unemployment has returned to Britain in a manner reminiscent of the inter-war years. Bevin's example in coping with similar circumstances is bound to be of great interest.

Despite massive opposition to trades unionism, and often

falling membership, and mass unemployment, he forged a positive and developing vision of practical trades unionism, pioneering what today we might call 'tripartism', demanding and winning in later years a recognised role for the voice of working people in the nation's affairs.

To the extent that such fundamental features of our society are being questioned today, Bevin's example is forceful and relevant.

Closely related to this was his achievement in the war years, a practical expression of the will of ordinary people to give of their best in the fight against Nazism and at the same time to better their own circumstances in so doing, and to lay the basis, not least in self-confidence, for the great social reforms which followed in the Attlee Government.

Though he sometimes faced criticism in those years, he was hailed by ordinary people as the peer of Churchill in his own field.

Though I never personally knew Bevin, my older colleagues – not least Frank Cousins and Jack Jones – frequently talked about Bevin, willing to learn from the Bevin years lessons which could be applied to the different circumstances of their own times.

While I am sure that some of Bevin's views and decisions would not have been appropriate in the circumstances, there has never been any question in the TGWU of the force of his heritage.

His honesty, common sense and intelligence were great qualities. His commitment to the working people's cause was never in doubt, and it should not be forgotten that he consistently refused honours and titles. And his alleged ruthlessness demands to be judged by the extremity of the situations which called it forth, while its harsher aspects did not seem to overflow into personal relations outside the pursuit of his work and duties as he saw them.

The views the author expresses are his own, and in no sense partisan to the trade union cause. His aim, and our aim, in publishing the book has been to provide the public with a new opportunity to read the remarkable story of the unskilled labourer who became a world statesman.

The book is not an attempt to write a history of the TGWU, or, indeed, to reflect the views of this great union. And because of the need to keep it to a reasonable length, it has not been possible to deal with many incidents and issues in great detail.

Nor has it been possible to describe the social conditions, the relationships between employers and working people, or political climates in detail or depth. There were many tough, bitter and desperate times for working people over the years in which Bevin was the leading spokesman for organised labour, and we should not forget that.

Finally, a note to the general reader. This book has been produced for public sale, not simply for distribution within our own ranks. A publication of this kind is a novel venture for us, and one of which Bevin would have approved, for it is unusual for unions in Britain to go into publishing in their own right.

If the book is a 'good read', that will be satisfaction enough for us as publishers, and, I am sure, for Mark Stephens. If it stimulates further re-appraisal of the Bevin years, that would be a welcome bonus.

Moss Evans, March 1981.

Chapter 1

Early Life

On 7 March 1951 the Foreign Office gave a birthday party for their Minister. Ernest Bevin was 70. They gave him a knee-hole desk, a dinner service and a huge birthday cake.

It was an unique event. Officially the Foreign Office only recognises the birthday of the reigning monarch, and nobody sends a present. On this occasion, however, every member of the Foreign Service from Bangkok to Washington, and from the rank of ambassador to the rank of messenger had each contributed a sixpenny piece.

To a man who had become a legend, it was also a singular tribute. The sixpenny pieces represented the 'full round orb of the dockers' tanner' won in the momentous Dock Strike of 1889, when 25,000 dockers peacefully marched through the City of London day in day out for three long, hot weeks and shamed their employers into giving them a penny an hour more.

In that year, as a direct result of the strike, the Dock, Wharf and Riverside Labourers' Union was formed; the union that Bevin was to join and later transform into the Transport and General Workers' Union. The contribution of a sixpenny piece was, therefore, both a fitting symbol of all that Bevin held most dear and a telling recognition of the source of his strength.

Diana Mercy Bevin was 40 years old when she gave birth for the last time in the Somerset village of Winsford on 7 March 1881. Ernest was her sixth son and her seventh child.

She had had a hard life. In the 1870s a flood of cheap wheat from the American prairies had driven thousands from the land in England, and amongst them the Bevins. Diana Bevin with her husband William had left their native Winsford with their bevy of children to seek work in South Wales. They were part of the second 'flight from the land'.*

There is no record of what happened to the Bevins in Wales. In 1877 however Diana Bevin returned to Winsford with all her children, but without her husband. From then on she described herself as a widow.

To keep herself and her family she undertook every job she could find: she was the village midwife; to several homes and farms she provided domestic help; and at the village inn, 'The Royal Oak', she helped in the kitchen.

Her only consolation was her burning faith. She was a staunch Nonconformist and every Sunday she worshipped at the Methodist tin hall in the village. In later years, in so far as she had any spare time, she spent it in raising money for the building of a brick chapel.

This was the world into which Ernest Bevin was born 100 years ago. It was a village world of great poverty where the poor, with almost no contact with the outside world, took care of each other until they could hold on no longer and then they left for the cities. It was a world where those with spirit became Nonconformists to indicate their independence, their rejection of the 'Establishment' and its hierarchies, and their right to be treated equally before God.

So when Ernest was born illegitimate (Diana Bevin never revealed who his father was), his mother did not hide him or treat him differently to any of her other children. She treasured him and did her best for him. From the age of three she sent him to the Methodist Sunday School, where in a velvet suit and a straw sailor's hat he used to give out the hymn books. Later she sent him to the village school in spite of the fact that it was a 'church' school.

Tragically at the beginning of 1889 Diana Bevin, suffering from a fibrous growth, was compelled to take to her bed. On

* The first 'flight from the land' occurred in the eighteenth century, a direct result of increased demand for labour in industry, and reduced demand for labour on farms due to improved farming techniques.

1 May she died, leaving the eight-year-old Ernie an orphan. The deep bond of affection between mother and youngest son of which he often spoke had been broken. He was alone.

After the funeral, to which all the villagers came, his half-sister Mary and her husband George Pope, a railwayman, undertook responsibility for him. Together they returned with Ernie to their home at Morchard Bishop in Devon.

The Popes did not remain long at Morchard Bishop. In the Autumn they moved to Copplestone and lived in a house called 'Tiddly Winks'. For three years they took good care of their charge, ensuring that he attended both school and chapel regularly. They did not pamper him. Before leaving for school the Popes expected him to help in the cottage, peeling potatoes and cleaning the family's shoes.

Both potato peeling and shoe cleaning were to feature later. For the Shaw Inquiry* he prepared a docker's dinner to put before the Judge and with his eye on the value of publicity had himself photographed peeling the potatoes, clad in long apron.

He turned his shoe cleaning activities to even better advantage. When stationed with Churchill in a special train at Droxford to watch the troops prepare for the invasion of Normandy in 1944, Churchill discovered that the Minister of Labour and National Service – as Bevin then was – cleaned his own shoes. Horrified that the man responsible for mobilising the entire country had to look after himself, Churchill gave instructions for Bevin to have a batman. Bevin was not keen. 'I wouldn't like you to do that, Prime Minister,' he said, 'I get such splendid ideas when I'm cleaning my boots.'

This story is born out by another. When Foreign Secretary he told M. Molotov that an idea for breaking a deadlock at a Foreign Ministers' Conference had come to him while cleaning his boots that morning. When the Soviet Minister expressed astonishment that the Foreign Minister of the United Kingdom should spend his time on so menial a task Bevin

* See photograph.

15

told him that it was most helpful to objective thinking and suggested that Molotov adopt the practice. Nobody knows whether Molotov did.

Then at the age of 11, when he had learnt to read, write and do his sums to a reasonable level, the Popes found him a living-in job at a nearby farm called Chaffcombe. Here the young Bevin worked ten hours a day six days a week for sixpence a week, payable every three months. It was a pitifully small wage compared, for example, to the 3s 6d per week that the nine-year-old Keir Hardie earned at a bakery in Central Glasgow 20 years before. But, Bevin did have unlimited access to the kitchen, where he was well fed.

For his sixpence a week he cut up mangolds and turnips, picked up stones, constructed bird scarers, hoed, dibbled and did any job required. In the evenings he was called upon to read out bits of news and leading articles from the *Bristol Mercury* to his master and his family by the kitchen fire. It was his first encounter with politics and the first opportunity he had ever had to put to some use the little education he had received.

In the winter of 1892–3 he had a chance of a better job in Copplestone itself where a farmer called May offered him full board and a shilling a week – twice the sum he was getting at Chaffcombe. But it turned out to be less congenial than his first job. After a row with his employer about the inadequate amount of cattle food he had chopped one morning (which some Copplestone villagers claim ended up with the terrified farmer hiding in a cupboard, so frightened was he of the young Bevin), Ernie came to the conclusion that farm work was not for him. He decided that he would prefer to try his hand at something else, should the opportunity present itself.

So when his brother Jack wrote to him in 1894 urging him to come to Bristol, Bevin left Copplestone to seek his fortune in the big city to which his other five brothers had already moved.

Chapter 2

Bristol

Bevin must have taken the train from Copplestone to Exeter St David's and under the shadow of the magnificence of Exeter Cathedral changed both platforms and railway company for the express to Bristol. Then travelling third class on hard wooden seats, the Great Western Railway would have taken him north-east through the Vale of Taunton.

The 76 miles between the two cities would have taken much the same time as it does today. Within less than two hours the train that was carrying the 13-year-old to a new life would be drawing into Bristol Temple Meads Station with its cathedral-like hammer-beam roof and its imposing turrets, buttresses and battlements, designed by that colossus of the railway age Isambard Kingdom Brunel 50 years before.

As he emerged from the station into Victoria Street (the very heart of what was then the Second City in the British Isles), Bristol must have been a stark and stimulating contrast to Copplestone. Above all, the clatter of carts rattling over the cobblestones and the milling crowds at this focal point would have shaken to the core anybody who had only known the peace of the countryside.

Having only a few shillings in his pocket, what Bevin needed was work; and work immediately. In this he was fortunate. His brother Albert, apprentice pastry cook at the Priory Restaurant in St Augustine's Parade, had managed to secure him a job in the bakehouse. For his labours he was to be paid six shillings a week plus meals.

It was an utterly menial job. For 12 hours a day he washed up, scrubbed floors and ran errands. The daily delivery of pies and pastries to the refreshment rooms of Temple Meads Station was his only relief to this dull routine. Moreover to a child of the fields, the hot atmosphere, the greasy smells and the disgusting jobs led him to seek a new job as quickly as he could find one.

What is significant and slightly puzzling at this stage of his career is that he never attempted to learn a skill. In spite of the fact that some of his brothers had learnt a trade, and that having a skill reduced the likelihood of unemployment, he never sought an apprenticeship. It is true that he would have found it difficult to break through the tightly-knit family circles which surrounded skilled trades but it appears that the thought never occurred to him that he might have the ability to acquire a skill.

Instead until 1901, he moved from job to job in a way that in retrospect appears both listless and irresponsible. For a few months he worked as a drayman. Then he worked in a buttershop. Then he returned to the Priory Restaurant as a pageboy. For the Bristol Tramways Co. he clipped tickets on the Horfield route which ran up past his home at Bishopston.

At one stage he must have worked in a laundry since as Foreign Secretary he claimed to have invented a method of ironing ostrich feathers on ladies' hats which earned him a special bonus. At the time of the siege of Mafeking he was unemployed for eight weeks, and it is thought that he was unemployed on a number of other occasions too.

Not until he became a carter for G. C. King in 1901 did he indicate any desire to settle down in a steady job. Then having become one of Mr King's permanent deliverers of mineral waters and having undertaken not to leave his employment in less than 12 months or to be concerned with 'the manufacture of mineral water cordials, syrups or hop bitters' within a radius of five miles from York Street, Bevin went on working for King's until 1906.

This job had a great deal to recommend it. It was an outdoor job. Bevin had to groom his own horse. Once loaded up and away from the works, he was his own master. For Bevin this was a good compromise between his country background and his desire for knowledge of the town. Moreover as he was paid a bonus of a penny a gross on all empty bottles he had a chance to earn something above his standard wage of 18 shillings a week.

One of the reasons for his indifference to learning a trade was his involvement in the church. After trying out a number of chapels, Bevin eventually committed himself to the Manor Hall Baptist Mission, a militant, evangelistic church which at one time boasted a Sunday school of almost 600 children.

In this church Bevin became fully involved. He distributed tracts, visited the sick and spoke at open air meetings as well as helped to run the Sunday School. On 5 January 1902 he was baptised by total immersion with 11 other members of the Mission at the Bethesda Chapel in Great George Street.

Bevin's time with the Mission was a key element in his development. It taught him to think. It taught him to speak in public. It imbued in him a strong sense of duty and a conviction that anything based on the Christian principles taught by the Nonconformists must be right. Besides, it also hovered on the edge of politics, as such giants of the cloth as the Rev. James Moffat Logan inveighed fiercely from the pulpit against the country's part in the Boer War while Bevin sat at his feet in his Sunday afternoon classes in the Old King Street Baptist Church.

The other ruling passion of his life was Florence Townley, the daughter of a wine taster at a Bristol wine merchants. After a fairly long courtship, they married secretly without ceremony and set up home in Saxon Road, in the district of St Warburgh's. Apparently Florence's influence had an immediate effect on Ernie: he became less aggressive and more fun. On Saturday nights, instead of going to a religious or political meeting, they both went down to the local Music Hall and joined in the singing. It was a practice they kept up until the beginning of the Second World War, when his job as Minister of Labour and National Service left him no time for such indulgences.

*

As Bevin toured the streets of Bristol in his carter's cap and green baize apron at horse's pace he had time and opportunity to see how the city and its outlying districts fitted together. What he saw was a wide range of riches and poverty which both surprised and angered him. In cruel contrast the elegance and show of the Edwardian Age in the fashionable city of Bristol only served to highlight the dilemma of those without, particularly the newly-arrived country folk with whom Bevin would have so closely identified.

The more he toured the streets and villages, the more 'the centre of his interest began to move away from the pulpit to the Bristol Socialist Society', to use Francis Williams' words in his biography of Bevin. He attended the Society's meetings, gradually adopted their views, and then became a paid-up member. He read their books, such as *Riches and Poverty* by Leo Chiozza Money which demonstrated the unequal division of the national income, and he longed for, and called for, action.

He recognised that the inequality that he surveyed from his cart was not just the inequality of wealth, but also of health, education and security. From then onwards, for the rest of his life, he identified with those who claimed to have found in Socialism an alternative method of social organisation which would rid the country of the evils which demeaned it.

In fact by joining the Bristol Socialist Society he had chosen the way of revolution, as the Bristol Society was part of the Social Democratic Federation which preached the overthrow of the existing order. So, it is most likely that at this stage in his career he believed that the rich and the privileged would have to be forced to relinquish their power and wealth, and that there was no way in which they could be persuaded to share those advantages by democratic means.

However it would be misleading to depict Bevin even at this stage as a revolutionary who thought in terms of military organisation and barricades. On the contrary, however extreme, the Bristol Socialist Society had a reputation for a sense of fun. The Society had its own band, its own choir and its own songbook. That too appealed to Bevin, who alternated the hymns that he had learnt at chapel with the songs he had learnt from the Socialists as he drove his wagon home at night, singing at the top of his rolling baritone voice.

Paradoxically, while in the process of becoming a socialist, Bevin made his only foray into private enterprise. In March 1906 he gave up his job as a carter and not only took over the 'Cabin Cafe' for his employer, Mr King, but also set up a coffee stall on his own in Avon Street. But by 1908 we find him back in charge of a cart; this time for John Macey with whom he stayed until 1911.

His identification with those without skill, his desire to act upon Christian principles and his longing to apply Socialist solutions first came together and found expression in his involvement in the Bristol Right-to-Work Committee. Founded in 1908 in response to a fierce rise in unemployment in the area, the members of the Committee appointed Bevin their Secretary.

At first they proved a singularly ineffective body of no political consequence. Then as a result of two bold and imaginative moves by Bevin, they burst into local prominence. Eye witnesses tell both stories in Alan Bullock's book *The Life and Times of Ernest Bevin*.

One day early in 1908, when Bevin was on his daily round and besieged with thoughts about how to make the Right-to-Work campaign a success, he spotted A. E. Ellery, a Labour councillor, walking along the pavement in Market Street. Inspired by an idea, Bevin quickly drew his cart into the side and collared Councillor Ellery. 'Alf,' he said, 'we need more publicity for our Right-to-Work Committee. You're a city councillor; you get the Mayor to see us.'

A few days later Bevin was on his way to see the Lord Mayor and the Town Clerk together with a deputation of 20 unemployed men. In making his case, Bevin did not just present a catalogue of the effects of unemployment. He pointed out that 'there was in the city a good deal of public work which could be put in hand without delay. By doing this, a good deal of labour would be absorbed by men who were now unemployed.' He laid before the Lord Mayor a number of suggestions, including the construction of a lake in Eastville Park; a proposal which the Council acted upon later, and caused the locals to re-name it 'Bevin's Lake'.

More dramatic than this was his entry into Bristol Cathedral at the head of a procession of 400 unemployed men at the morning service on Sunday 9 November. According to Alderman Sheppard who took part, they were 'a ragged lot led by a ragged band playing "True to Death"', but in their behaviour wholly orderly, thanks to a little drilling from Bevin beforehand. Then interspersed between the silks and the crinolines, the soft velvets and the stout worsteds, they sat silently through the service: a vivid challenge to the middle class conscience of the Established Church. Much impressed by their plight, the Dean and Chapter were soon also agitating on their behalf to the City Council.

Little did they know that Bevin's aims were not wholly philanthropic, as a later meeting of the Right-to-Work Committee was to prove. At the annual Meeting of the Committee, Bevin said: '... nothing but a complete social and economic revolution is going to solve the problem. We must feed the people in order that men may be strong enough physically and mentally to carry out that revolution which will come at no distant date.'

Through such antics Bevin undoubtedly focused attention not only on the problem of unemployment but also on himself. So when he stood as Socialist and Labour candidate for St Paul's Ward in the municipal elections, the contest excited considerable local passion. In the event Bevin polled more votes than any previous winning candidate, but was still soundly beaten by the Liberal whose party machine had pulled out all the stops to defeat him.

Furious at the result and also suspicious of foul play, Bevin accused the Liberal Agent of infringing the law of secrecy that applies to ballots by divulging the identity of some of

Bevin's supporters. However Bevin lost his appeal and in high dudgeon returned to his mineral wagon.

Worse was to come. Now branded a red hot Socialist agitator, his political opponents managed to persuade a number of his customers to boycott his deliveries of mineral water, to help hound him out of Bristol. They were very nearly successful. His sales slumped and the dejected Bevin offered his resignation to his employer, believing this to be the only honourable course left open to him. But John Macey, his master, although a Liberal, would not hear of it. So Bevin stayed and between them they defeated the boycott.

All the same, the hostility that he had aroused had shaken Bevin to the core. In the course of 1910 he gave up the secretaryship of the Right-to-Work Committee and one of his friends remembers him talking about doing a theological course, possibly with a view to becoming a missionary and going overseas.

The desire to make a clean break did not last long. During the summer of 1910 Harry Orbell of the Dock, Wharf, Riverside and General Workers' Union asked Bevin to set up a local relief fund to help those dockers in difficulties as a result of a strike in Avonmouth and Bristol docks; on account of his proven ability as an organiser, and in spite of the fact that Bevin was not a member of the union himself.

From this contact it naturally followed that the dockers should ask him to become a member and also set up a branch of the union amongst the carters. In response to this invitation Bevin called a meeting of the local carters. First they resolved to set up a carmen's branch of the Dockers' Union; then they elected Bevin their chairman. They then all enrolled and received an illuminated certificate of membership dated 27 August 1910.

Just as the photograph of his mother was to hold pride of place behind his desk at Transport House, so his certificate of membership was to take pride of place over the fireplace at his home. He was 29 years old and still a manual worker,

23

whereas his future colleague Winston Churchill, aged 36, was already Home Secretary.

Joining the Dockers' Union and becoming chairman of the carters' branch was the most decisive step in Bevin's career. It set him on the path which was to lead him ultimately to become Foreign Secretary. As both manual worker and trade union representative Bevin had brought two key aspects of his personality together.

Not surprisingly, he was an outstanding success. Within six months he had enlisted 2,050 members into the carmen's branch: an amazing feat in such a short time, as there were few focal points where carters met and hundreds of firms for which they worked.

Bevin crowned this achievement by persuading the Bristol employers to recognise the Union and then negotiate an agreement for the industry locally. At a time when it was a common practice for employers to resist recognition and then take positive steps to break up a newly-formed union, particularly in an industry which had not been organised before, this made Bevin's achievement all the more remarkable.

Besides, by the standards of the time, it was a first class agreement. For a 67-hour week, a carter with two horses to look after was to have a wage of 26 shillings a week. In addition, to the detriment of both masters and men but to the evident advantage of the horses, all parties to the agreement undertook not to load up their wagons beyond the weight of three tons.

This aspect of the agreement, for which Bevin was wholly responsible, gave him particular satisfaction. As a countryman, the way some carters loaded their wagons to the breaking point of their horses' strength for the sake of a few coppers extra bonus had horrified him; so had the way that the employers encouraged and connived at this practice. Taking on both sides, he bullied them into agreement in a way that foreshadowed the Bevin of the future; and then, to add insult to injury, he made regular checks in the city to

24

ensure that the new rule was observed.

He was developing into a pugnacious, powerful leader who was beginning to sense the power that lay within him. No story illustrates his ruthless determination better than the case of the drayman sentenced to gaol for taking two apples from a waste bin on the wharf. Within an hour of hearing of the sentence Bevin was marching through the city at the head of a great company of dockers and carters with two apples impaled on the poles of the banner that declared their protest. He kept up his campaign until a re-trial was ordered.

Such a talent for getting results was too valuable to be restricted to part-time union work and in the Spring of 1911 Ben Tillett, General Secretary and one of the heroes of the 1889 Dock Strike, invited Bevin to become a full-time official in the Bristol area.

So at the age of 30 he climbed down from his cart for the last time and as Francis Williams says, 'entered upon his kingdom'.

The Summer of 1911 was the hottest and driest since records began in the Greenwich Observatory in 1841. At its peak the Observatory registered a temperature of 100°F in the shade. It heralded a wave of industrial unrest which rose to a crescendo in 1912 when 40 million working days were lost in strikes – a total only exceeded in 1921 and 1926.

During a period of less than 18 months every port, every coalfield and every railway was on strike at one moment or another; in some cases, more than once. In 1911 in Liverpool, for example, at one moment every form of transport had come to a halt: trains, trams, carts and ships. In 1912 the crisis deepened when 200,000 railmen struck.

Bristol had its share of unrest, but there is no evidence to suggest that Bevin took much part in the strikes. Over the period it seems that he spent most of his time building up membership in South Wales and the South-West – in Cardiff so successfully that the members presented him with a gold watch and chain in appreciation of his hard work.

With new branches springing up in every corner of his territory, Bevin had made his mark and in 1913 Ben Tillett moved him to head office in the Mile End Road. Then when Harry Orbell died in March 1914, Bevin took his place as one of the three National Organisers. He was now one of the half dozen men at the head of his union.

One of Ben Tillett's remarkable creations was the National Transport Workers' Federation. The Federation consisted of 26 unions with a membership of 150,000 men which the mercurial Tillett had hurriedly welded together to provide a strike committee and a single public voice for the conduct of the London Dock Strike of 1911.

In spite of its divisions and inner conflicts he had managed to hold the Federation together and at its annual General Council Meeting in June 1913 a resolution calling on the Executive Council to prepare a scheme for the complete amalgamation of all members of the Federation had been carried with acclamation. This was the first meeting at national level that Bevin had ever attended, and what he heard of the grand plan of amalgamation matched with what he had already experienced on a small scale in Bristol.

This led him to speak powerfully at a special conference on amalgamation in Caxton Hall, Westminster, on 8 July 1914: 'I happen to be where the dockers and carters are in one union and there the carters have been more successful than in any other town in the country in relation to the conditions they were under before.'

He went on to explain that with a central executive representing a variety of trades, such co-operation gave them the power to negotiate. 'It is not so much that it means a power to attack,' he said, 'as a power to negotiate, and that power to negotiate is the most valuable thing that we can have.' The reason was obvious. 'Where there is practically one union covering all transport and the bulk of the general labourers' unions in one town, what is the first thing the employers ask? It is, "Will you all strike together?" '

Bevin's case was convincing. He had seen what prizes co-operation between trades could win. He had cited a glittering example. From now onwards he was to give all ideas of amalgamation and alliance his unstinting support; the vote of 26 unions in favour of being merged into one consolidated Union of Labour with only two against and two abstentions suggested that the rest of the movement was moving in this direction too.

But Britain's declaration of war against Germany during the Bank Holiday weekend in August 1914 brought all plans to a halt and when normal life resumed again four years later the world was a very different place, particularly for the trade unions and Ernest Bevin.

Chapter 3

First World War

There were a number of Socialists who hoped that any serious threat of war would inspire an international general strike. At least they had high hopes that the working people of Britain and Germany would join hands in fraternal unity and refuse to take up arms.

Amongst those who thought this way was Ernest Bevin. Over the weekend while the London Socialists were holding a massive anti-war rally in Trafalgar Square, Bevin was on a soapbox on the Bristol Downs roundly condemning militarism and urging all working people to refuse to do their government's bidding in the event of war.

But Germany's invasion of Belgium with the tacit support of the German Social Democratic Party and the German Trade Unions cut the ground from under the feet of the British Socialists. In response, in a matter of days the Labour Party, the TUC and the General Federation of Trade Unions formed a joint board and had declared both an industrial and political truce unilaterally and unconditionally. The Labour Party readily joined a coalition government in May 1915.

It was a remarkable reversal of policy and it enraged Bevin who dared to hit the only really sour note at the 1915 TUC at Bristol in, of all things, his maiden speech:

'What I want to get from the representatives of the Labour Party,' he said in his forthright, pugilistic way, 'is some indication of the exact position they found themselves in at the outbreak of war.... I do not take any notice of what Mr Ramsay MacDonald on the one hand, or Mr John Hodge on the other, may say. I want to know what happened when the Labour Party was called upon to make its decision....'

In his work, however, Bevin was never obstructive. Throughout the war he did his utmost to prevent disputes and to keep goods and munitions flowing through the ports. For someone with such little experience of politics, he pursued a surprisingly distinctive and independent line. On the one hand, he condemned the pacifists; on the other, he criticised the Labour members in the Coalition Government for not getting a better deal for labour. For instance, at the Bristol TUC he proposed that the Government should create a Minister of Labour and give him full Cabinet rank; an uncanny foretaste of things to come.

Of all the experiences that Bevin had during the First World War the one that had the greatest impact on his thinking and outlook was his visit to the United States of America in the Autumn of 1915. It was his first trip abroad.

The visit had emanated from that same TUC Conference at which Bevin had made his startling maiden speech. One of Conference's tasks was to elect a fraternal delegate from among their number for the annual convention of the American Federation of Labour (AFL). Normally it was considered a special honour. But in 1915 the U-boat attacks were at their height (they had sunk the *Lusitania* in May) and amongst the longer serving members there was only one volunteer.

For the second place, a hasty search was made for nominations. Bevin leapt at the chance. Duly elected, on 12 October he boarded the SS *Orduna* with Charlie Ammon of the Post Office Workers bound for New York.

Their first official task was to attend the ceremony to mark the opening of the AFL's new headquarters. Eight storeys high it made a deep impression on Bevin. 'In all Britain, even in London itself, there is no building worthy of so great a movement as that of the organised workers,' he wrote home a little enviously, and from then on dreamt of something as imposing in the heart of London for his own Union.

Samuel Gompers, the President of the AFL, was a flamboyant, shrewd, tough character who had become the grandee of the American labour scene. Originally a cigarmaker from London, he had first been elected President of the AFL in

1882; then from 1895 until his death in 1924 he was re-elected President each year without a break. In Bevin's eyes Gompers appeared almost as impressive as his building.

In outlook Gompers was the very antithesis of Bevin: fiercely anti-socialist and pro-craft-unionism. In character, however, they were much the same, and they became firm friends while travelling across the continent by train to San Francisco. Bevin particularly admired the way that Gompers treated the heads of the big American Corporations as equals and yet at the same time squeezed out of them the very best terms and conditions for his members.

At the end of the fortnight's convention, Gompers presented Bevin with a gift: a heavy gold ring embossed with the figure of a naked lady. As he tried to press it onto the finger of one of Bevin's massive hands, he found it was far too small. 'What's that you got – a bunch of bananas?' Gompers remarked, amazed at their size.

This story epitomises the difference between the backgrounds of the two men: the difference between the delicate art of rolling a cigar and the brute force needed to shift a crate of mineral water bottles; and Bevin delighted in it. He treasured the ring, wore it to the end of his life and used it to seal the North Atlantic Treaty on behalf of the United Kingdom in 1949.

Above all, the visit to America stretched Bevin's imagination and made him look at the drift of world events in larger and wider terms. In the last of the six articles which he wrote for the *Dockers' Record* in 1916 he summed up his visit in these terms:

'To me it was a source of education. It broadened my views in conception of the great world problems: it indicated as we met representatives of the different races and creeds, how akin we were in human desires, weaknesses and ideas; it emphasised that the need of the workers was a common one, that the struggle was a common one, that the enemy was a common one; and it made one long for the time when the world to the workers will be as small as it is to the capitalists; when the common intelligence of the workers will develop to the same degree as the capitalists' intelligence to exploit it.'

In that packed paragraph, bulging with ideas, Bevin seems to have encapsulated much of what he was to fight for during the rest of his life.

Otherwise Bevin's war was an endless round of meetings and conferences. But as the number of trade unionists increased (from 4 million to 6½ million during the war), so the form of many negotiations changed.

Before the change occurred, wage negotiations took place locally. Not only did this mean that officials like Bevin were in perpetual motion, as they travelled from conference to conference, but also that their negotiating power was only as strong as their local membership.

To Bevin this arrangement seemed to nullify the advantages of being affiliated to the same organisation such as the National Transport Workers' Federation. And, of course, the case for the presentation of joint claims was basically the same as the case for amalgamation.

Nobody saw the advantages of a joint claim more clearly than Bevin and in August 1917 at a conference in Salford of 17 members of the Transport Workers' Federation, Bevin proposed that they present 50 similar claims simultaneously at 50 different locations. The unions agreed, the motion was carried and the claims submitted.

This posed the employers a dilemma. Did they negotiate separately and face the prospect of orchestrated disruption, should they fail to reach a settlement? Or did they opt for one general negotiation to cover all claims? After much deliberation they decided upon the latter and eventually reached agreement with the carters, lorrymen and motormen through the services of Sir George Askwith, the Chief Industrial Commissioner.

This is exactly what Bevin hoped might happen. For the first time in history a large and disparate group of unskilled workers, within a federation, had negotiated a national agreement. With this pioneering success behind him, Bevin then managed to do the same for the tram and bus workers and also for the dockers. The case for amalgamation was gradually getting stronger.*

In the 'khaki' election which followed so quickly after the war that only one in four of the returning troops were able to vote, Bevin stood against the Coalition candidate at Bristol Central. Because he stood against the Coalition and, in particular, roundly denounced the popular cry of 'Making Germany pay', he was accused in turn of being a bolshevik, a pacifist and pro-German.

In fact all he was trying to do, in his commonsense way, was to get his electorate to think about how on earth the bankrupt Germans could pay; a sentiment which, paradoxically, he shared with Lloyd George. But in company with MacDonald, Snowden and even Henderson, Bevin lost heavily. Bevin's decision thereafter for the next 20 years not to seek a political career was as decisive as his decision 20 years earlier not to learn a trade. It left him free to build up what was to become the largest unskilled and semi-skilled trade union in the world.

The two years that followed were deeply troubled. Between October 1918 and the Spring of 1919 revolutions broke out in Germany, Austria and Hungary and in the expectation that these would spread, the Third Communist International† was founded in Moscow in March 1919.

The whole of central Europe was in a state both of collapse and of political instability; in Britain the unrest expressed itself in strikes on a scale not seen in this country either before or since, except in 1926, the year of the General Strike. Again, as in 1911 and 1912, Bevin does not seem to have been personally involved.

But he was very directly involved in the development of the

* See below, Chapter 6.
† The First Socialist International was founded in 1864; the Second in 1889, the Centenary of the French Revolution. The International referred to here was founded by the Communists.

Triple Alliance of miners, railwaymen and transport workers, originally proposed by the miners at the beginning of 1914. On paper the Alliance looked a powerful instrument, strong enough to take on any government whose actions cut across the interests of the trade unions. It represented 1½ million trade unionists, one sixth of the adult male labour of the entire nation.

At the outset while unity was not put to the test, it appeared successful: the miners won a temporary increase; the railwaymen prevented a sizeable reduction in wages being implemented; all branches of the Alliance won a reduction in hours. To the general public it appeared an unassailable giant, and they attributed these successes to its existence. But Bevin was never satisfied with its organisation.

'It is a great shapeless mass, all the time struggling to co-ordinate its efforts but finding itself without a head to direct,' he wrote in the *Daily Herald* on 17 July 1919. 'There is no national body representing the whole of the trade unions of the country with any real directive authority – co-ordinating claims and policy; marshalling all the forces of Labour; adopting methods to educate its membership . . . ; ready to inaugurate a campaign which would rally all its political and industrial forces in order to fight the vested interests.'

Bevin was never satisfied with the arrangements, because in his view the Triple Alliance had never effectively operated. It was not the negotiating body he wanted. It had never acted in concert, and no individual union had ever consulted its other members before either striking or settling.

What Bevin wanted were more effective arrangements for acting together through the TUC. He was not alone in this, and in the Autumn of 1919 the TUC created a co-ordination sub-committee with Bevin as one of its members to consider the possibility of joint action.

The conclusions reached by the Sub-Committee were to change the course of trade union history and create a structure within the TUC which broadly exists today. Based on a memo dated 19 November 1919, written by Ernest Bevin, the Sub-

Committee recommended that a general council replace the Parliamentary Committee with responsibility for looking after not only the legislative but also the economic interests of its members.

Divided into nine groups and totalling approximately 30 members, the Council was to represent the whole Movement. The General Council was to have power to 'co-ordinate industrial action'. It was to 'promote common action by the Trade Union Movement on general questions such as wages and hours of labour', and was to have 'power to assist any union which is attacked on any vital question of trade union principle'. It was to use its influence to help settle inter-union disputes and it was to enter into relations with other trade union movements 'with a view to promoting common action and international solidarity'.

Presented to a special TUC Conference on 9 and 10 December, this report was to alter radically the standing and effectiveness of the TUC. In one sense, it changed nothing in that individual unions still held sovereign right to do what they thought was best for their members. In another sense, it transformed the standing and potential power of the TUC by creating a general staff which at any moment could be called upon to lead the Movement into battle.

Once again Bevin had proved himself the architect of organisation, the master builder of the Movement. At much the same time as his fertile brain was propounding ways of constructing a general council, his organisational mind was delving into an entirely different field – that of journalism.

At the end of November he wrote three articles for the *Daily Herald* entitled 'The Written Word'. His aim was to inspire support for a Labour press. Nothing could illustrate better the value he set on a powerful Labour daily than this passage:

'The first and most important thing is to stir, enlighten, organise the minds of the people. Physical poverty will remain as long as there is mental poverty. There is, at this moment, in the world less apathy than bewilderment; and therefore the whole of the people's position needs clarifying.

'The spoken word has been a mighty factor in the past. But it is not enough. We must have the written word daily. It is as essential as a political instrument or the strike weapon. It is needed to make either of these effective.'

That same November a *Daily Herald* trade union committee was set up, with Bevin as Secretary. Largely thanks to his efforts, it raised £100,000. It was the beginning of a 20-year association with the *Daily Herald* which in later life Bevin was to call 'my paper'.

Chapter 4

Dockers' KC

Until 1920 Bevin had no national standing. In Bristol and within the union movement he was relatively well known. During the war Lloyd George had offered him a minor post as Labour Adviser (which he had turned down) and he had served on a number of national committees. But in no sense was he a national figure.

Overnight the part Bevin played in the Shaw Inquiry launched him into the forefront of the public gaze. It was a turning point in his career and a turning point in the history of Labour.

The Shaw Inquiry had come about like this. The country's 125,000 dockers had tabled a comprehensive claim against the employers for a higher day rate, improved overtime and shift rates and a guaranteed wage. Instead of rejecting the claim and insisting upon local negotiations the employers proposed a public inquiry which they were entitled to do under legislation passed two months before.*

This put the dockers in a dilemma. They had little confidence that the Inquiry would treat them fairly and expected the composition of the Court to be loaded against them. Amongst the members of the Transport Workers Federation they would never get agreement to instruct the best barrister in the land to represent them. Yet they wanted to repeat the success that the tramwaymen and carters had had through their national negotiations.

What were the unions to do? Was their case strong enough? The Transport Workers Federation hesitated and then at a meeting of their full General Council on 30 December 1919, decided to take a risk and participate. At the same meeting they elected Bevin to represent them.

* The Industrial Courts Act, 1919.

It was to be the first Inquiry of its kind. Its purpose was to examine the evidence put forward by both sides and then to make recommendations. Lord Shaw of Dunfermline, a High Court Judge and one-time radical member of parliament, was to preside over the proceedings – hence the name 'Shaw Inquiry'.

To prepare, Bevin had only just over one month. In that time he had to master his brief, organise and rehearse witnesses, and assemble a vast range of statistics to prove the employers' ability to pay and the dockers' inability to cope on present earnings. For help he had the meagre resources of the Dockers' Union, the Federation and the unstinting support of his secretary Mae Forcey, formerly a publicity agent for a theatrical impresario, whose unquenchable thirst for research was to pay handsome dividends.

On 3 February 1920 the Inquiry opened at the Law Courts in the Strand. As the origin of the Inquiry was the Unions' claim, Lord Shaw's first task was to ask Bevin to make the opening statement on behalf of the Unions.

'The Court will appreciate,' Bevin began, 'that this is an unusual environment for me to be in and also that the proceedings are very novel for the whole Labour movement of this country. We have agreed as transport workers to submit our claims to the test of public inquiry, first because we are convinced of the justice of our claim, and secondly because we have no objection to the whole question of the standard of life being open for public inquiry. We hope it will serve not only to obtain what our men desire but to influence public opinion to a higher conception of what that standard of life ought to be.'

Bevin's opening statement lasted 11 hours and spread over three days. He traced the history of the dockers, the conditions under which they worked, the profits which both the Port Authorities and the shipowners had made during the War and both the inadequacy and irregularity of the wages the dockers received.

Newspaper reports say that he never lost the thread of his

argument and never repeated himself. For someone who had had so little education, no legal training and had only given up manual work at the age of 30, this was an extraordinary achievement. It amazed both public and court alike.

On the one hand, he showed how the capital value of ships had soared and in passing quoted the admission of Bonar Law, in the House of Commons, that in the last year of the War he had made a 47% profit on his shipping shares. On the other, he explained how the value of the docker's wage had halved since 1905.

Then he went into the details of the cost of his proposals. In words that express the eternal and universal fear of working people throughout the world, Bevin condemned the casual labour system, saying: 'I am convinced that the employers have always had at the back of their heads that economic poverty producing economic fear was the best weapon for controlling labour. I do not think that civilisation built upon that is worth having.'

As he reached the climax of his speech, in a magnificent tirade Bevin concluded:

'I suggest that your Court cannot refuse our claim either on grounds of equity or of reason. If the captains of industry who have claimed monopoly control for themselves, who have argued that we are not capable of taking part in control, say that they are unable to organise their concerns so as to give us work for a decent standard of life, then I say that they ought to lose their places .... By whatever means they have got control, there comes with it responsibility; and if they cannot improve the organisation of industry then I say they ought to make way.'

The final words of his opening statement expressed all the pain and pent-up frustration of his class:

'If your Court refuse our claim, I suggest you must adopt an alternative. You must go to the Prime Minister, you must go to the Minister of Education and tell him to close our schools, tell him that industry can only be run by artisan labour on the pure fodder or animal basis, teach us nothing,

38

let us learn nothing, because to create aspirations in our minds, to create the love of the beautiful and then at the same time to deny us the wherewithal to obtain it, is a false policy and a wrong method to adopt. Better keep us in dark ignorance, never to know anything, if you are going to refuse us the wherewithal to give expression to those aspirations which have thus been created.'

After being congratulated by the Judge, Bevin sat down to thunderous applause and awaited the employers' counter-attack. For the employers Sir Lynden Macassey KC replied. The proposal for a national minimum wage was wholly impracticable. In conditions, wages and trade practices the differences between ports were too great. Like the mineowners, the Port Authorities were quite prepared to have district negotiations, but not national negotiations. To provide a common wage for all dockers would have severe repercussions and would probably disturb the wage structure of the whole country.

Bevin, Sir Lynden argued, had exaggerated both the straits of the dockers and the rise in the cost of living. The figure of £6 a week, which Bevin had suggested that a family of five needed, was far too high. A more appropriate figure would be £3 12s 6d.

This assertion gave rise to the most dramatic incident in the Inquiry. To justify his figure of £3 12s 6d, Macassey called Professor A. L. Bowley, who held the Chair of Statistics at London University, as an expert witness. In a clinical and unfeeling way Bowley explained to the Court how he had made up his shopping basket.

This approach enraged Bevin, particularly as he had no means of challenging Bowley on similar academic grounds. But it also gave him an idea: to produce the food itself as a silent witness.

So early the following morning Mae Forcey and Ernest Bevin went shopping in a street market in Canning Town. They bought exactly the amount of vegetables, cheese and meat allowed for in Professor Bowley's housekeeping budget for a docker's family of five. Then the two returned to the Union's headquarters just off the Strand to cook their purchases.*

Laying out five plates in front of the Judge, Bevin began: 'I ask the Court, my Lord, to examine the dinner which Counsel for the Employers considers adequate to sustain the strength of a docker hauling 71 tons of wheat a day on his back.' (Later he pointed out that a horse pulled only 50 tons a week.)

Then he called a witness, a docker from Birkenhead, and asked him what would happen, 'if you went home from the dock to a meal like that and you were told by your wife that Counsel said there was sufficient calorific value in it to sustain you? What would be the result?'

'I think the dockers would emigrate in a body,' the docker replied.

But Bevin had not quite defeated Bowley. Professor Bowley suggested that a really responsible docker's wife – the 'greatest chancellor of the exchequer that ever lived', as Bevin described her – could buy food of high calorific value at low prices, if she so chose. So the following day Bevin presented a 'ration' of bacon on five plates, and the day after six pennyworth of fish.

For every meagre offering Professor Bowley had an explanation. Not until Bevin produced a 7 shillings menu from the Savoy for the sort of meal that an 'ordinary' shipowner might eat did he manage to silence the irrepressible Professor with the question: 'What is the calorific value of that when he has eaten it?'; and from the Professor answer came there none.

The presentation of a succession of meals in court was a brilliant visual device which caught the imagination of the public and in terms of publicity was unsurpassable. Photographs of the meagre portions of food appeared in half a dozen papers over the caption of 'A docker's breakfast'. This was strangely reminiscent of the 1889 Strike when the meagre

* See photograph.

'Docker's dinner' was held high on a pike next to the ample 'Sweater's dinner' during one of the demonstrations in the City.

Although the shopping basket contest between Bevin and Bowley took place over a number of days, the contestants spent most of the time of the Inquiry presenting intricate details to support their arguments: the extent of extra money paid for 'dirty' cargoes at Avonmouth, for instance.

For 20 days the contest raged with submissions followed by counter-submissions, and examinations followed by cross-examinations. Neither side gave an inch, but all the time in the public's eyes Bevin's stature grew through his dogged determination to match the intellect of one of the country's most brilliant lawyers.

In his closing speech, Bevin gathered all the principal aspects of the dockers' claim together, highlighting the need for a national scheme of registration and maintenance (guaranteed wage):

'I want the Court to declare for the principle of maintenance. The reason is this.... Take education. This State did not build all the schools and then say all the children should be educated. Parliament declared that it was essential that children should be educated and then proceeded to build the structure. I want the same principle adopted here.'

Finally in a voice full of emotion he concluded:

'I appeal to you, whatever the economic circumstances may be – surely, my Lord, justice cannot be dependent upon consequences. If the claim I have made is just, then the consequences of its granting must follow and be met.'

From Lord Shaw, Bevin's performance evoked an immediate response:

'Mr Bevin, at the close of your opening speech I felt authorised by the feeling of the Court to express our satisfaction with it. That satisfaction has not lessened during the course of these proceedings.... Be assured that whatever the result be, the Court will be unanimous in this: that you shall get justice, nothing more nor less than justice, in this case. We congratulate you on the cogent and impressive address which you have now delivered.'

Even before the announcement of the result, the dockers celebrated Bevin's triumph. On 7 March they marched from Temple Station to the Albert Hall. There they acclaimed their hero. In response Bevin said:

'This Court of Inquiry, novel as it is, curious as it may be taken as a method of settling a dispute, is something bigger than merely an inquiry into 16 shillings a day. It has been a platform on which it has been possible to open a page of history that tells of the struggles of the men and women we represent. It has been an opportunity to unfold the great human tragedy of men and women fighting year in year out against the terrible economic conditions with which they have been surrounded. Although my speech took 11 hours, let me say that no tongue exists, no voice is capable, no pen can write, no artist can paint, the real human tragedy that is behind it all.'

Then he enunciated a principle which he believed lay at the heart of trade unionism: 'When the time comes, if it ever does, for a great struggle between Capital and Labour, I want it to be for something bigger than a penny an hour .... I want it to have a very definite object – that of achieving for those who toil the mastery of their own lives.'

Three weeks later the Court re-assembled to deliver its verdict. By a majority decision the Court condemned the system of casual labour, declared for registration and the principle of maintenance and awarded a national minimum of 16 shillings a day for a 44-hour week.

From the Court the dockers had won everything for which they had asked. In the negotiations which followed on the subject of implementation they were almost equally successsful. With the single exception of maintenance and in spite of some very real complications, the employers accepted the Award in full. For maintenance Bevin had to wait until 1941, when he had the satisfaction of introducing it into the docks as Minister of Labour.

Of all the momentous events in Bevin's life, the Shaw Inquiry stands out as the most momentous. From a position of relative obscurity within a union of medium size, over the 20 days of the Inquiry Bevin had established himself as the most powerful union leader in the country. Northcliffe's *Daily Mail* said that he had 'pegged out for himself a place in the front rank of men who count in social politics'.

But at the same time as Bevin rose to become a leader, so he lifted the Movement with him. As Lord Bullock says in his book about Bevin, 'the inquiry had become an indictment of the industrial system which allowed such conditions to continue and he himself the spokesman of the whole working class.... It was his, and his audience's, sense of his role that gave his advocacy its curiously dramatic quality.'

Dubbed the 'Dockers' KC' by the *Daily Herald*, his role had really been wider than that. For the first time a working man had compelled the employers and the nation not only to listen to the working man's anger and resentment over his conditions and status but also to do something about it immediately.

This proved, in the most vivid way, that there was a means of effecting a massive change in circumstances for working people without immediate resort to the strike weapon. It was a lesson to which Bevin constantly referred later, a lesson which changed the direction of his revolutionary fervour and confirmed his belief in the power of negotiation.

For Bevin his personal circumstances changed at this time too. Over the Shaw Inquiry his wife Flo and six-year-old daughter Que* came to London. After living in several flats they eventually settled in a small house in Golders Green where they stayed for the rest of the 1920s. When the Dockers' Union appointed Bevin Assistant General Secretary in May and raised his salary to £650 a year they were able to live comfortably and together for the first time since Bevin had left Bristol.

* Christened Queenie, called Que – now Mrs Sydney Wynne.

Chapter 5

Council of Action

The Russian Revolution evoked considerable sympathy from the Labour Movement in 1917. They saw it as an end to the most oppressive tyranny in Europe. In particular Lenin's call for 'Peace, Land, and Bread', the introduction of workers' control and the end of private trade inspired them.

So when Poland, one of the few beneficiaries of the re-writing of the European map at the end of the War, invaded Russia, the Labour Movement was on the side of the 'Red Army'. But, with minimal political clout, there seemed little that Labour could do about it.

On the face of it Britain was neutral. She had withdrawn from Russian soil the few remaining troops she had there. But the suspicion lingered in Labour circles that the Coalition Government would be mightily relieved, if the Poles helped speed the demise of Bolshevism.

In April 1920 crates with the label 'OHMS Munitions for Poland' roused the suspicions of a group of dockers in London's East India Dock. Required to load them onto the *Jolly George*, a Watford Line boat, they decided to dispatch a deputation to Ernest Bevin before undertaking to do so.

Unhesitatingly Bevin ruled that the Union would support the dockers officially if they took action. Consequently the *Jolly George* had to leave the Thames without the British Government's delivery of military equipment for the Polish army on board.

In itself it was a small incident. Nonetheless in the history of trade unionism it was significant. For the first time trade unionists had deliberately used their industrial muscle for political purposes.

At the Triennial Delegate Conference at Plymouth in May, Bevin congratulated the dockers on their bold move, and then justified the line he took. Basing his case on the principle that working people have a right to say where and how their labour should be used, he said: 'Whatever may be the merits or demerits of the theory of government of Russia, that is a matter for Russia, and we have no right to determine their form of government, any more than we would tolerate Russia determining our form of government.'

Here was a statesman-like approach. Bevin was outlining the principle of self-determination. He was not declaring support for a particular political system. This is an important point. A Labour deputation to Russia had just returned with a fearful report of conditions there – famine, disease and especially the total absence of carbolic soap.* The Poles were still advancing and were about to capture Kiev. Yet Bevin presented a case of principle, not of political preference.

Then the tide turned. The 'Red Army' chased the Poles out of Russia, and pushed into Poland. By the beginning of August the roar of Communist artillery was heard in the streets of Warsaw. *The Times* spoke of war as imminent, declaring: 'We must face it with the same unanimity and the same courage with which we faced the crisis of 1914.'

This stung the Labour Movement into action. The *Daily Herald* produced a special Sunday edition with the headline: 'Not a Man, Not a Gun, Not a Sou', and Bevin called for a meeting between the three arms of the Labour Movement: the TUC, the Labour Party Executive and the Parliamentary Labour Party.

The Conference took place on 9 August and immediately formed a 'council of action'. In spite of the fact that he was not a member of any of the three bodies concerned, the Council appointed Bevin its spokesman.

With British warships already in the Baltic and Marshal Foch under orders to draw up plans for invasion on behalf of both British and French Governments, a second major European war seemed inevitable. To register their heartfelt

* Carbolic soap contains a basic antiseptic. Without it people were vulnerable to disease.

dissent and the support of 6 million trade unionists, the Council asked for an immediate meeting with Lloyd George, the Prime Minister.

The meeting took place next day. Lloyd George was then at the height of his reputation and it was Bevin's first visit to 10 Downing Street. But Bevin, unimpressed by either the man or his surroundings, heaved the full weight of the Council's position at Lloyd George in his first few words: 'At the outset I want to make it perfectly clear that the resolution is not merely one in opposition to direct military action, but it is a declaration in opposition to what I would describe as an indirect war, either by blockade or by the supply of munitions or by assisting the forces that are now at war with Russia.'

Bevin emphasised the right of every country to make its own constitutional arrangements. 'The public declarations of Russia up to now are that they are not challenging the independence of Poland,' he said. Then he declared that the Council intended to see the Russian representatives in London to seek confirmation of this undertaking.

Once Lloyd George had acknowledged the force of their argument, the delegation left No. 10 and called a much bigger meeting of the Labour Movement at Central Hall, Westminster four days later. There before a thousand cheering representatives, Bevin declared:

'In the name of the British Labour Party, I say that no one man or set of men has the right to say that the honour of a country is at stake when the country does not know the facts. I hope Labour is going to fight this to the bitter end.... Our great work in life until now has been mainly wages, but I say in all sincerity that this question you are called upon to decide today – the willingness to take action to win world peace – transcends any claim in connection with wages or hours of labour.'

Resolution after resolution was passed unanimously, including one authorising the Council 'to call for any and every form of withdrawal of labour which circumstances may require.' Seldom has the Labour Movement presented such a perfect picture of unity.

Whether the threat altered the policy of Lloyd George is a matter for debate. Lloyd George insisted that the Government was going to remain neutral anyway. But the fact is that the British neither sent supplies nor arms to the Poles and it is most probable, as A. J. P. Taylor says in his Oxford History of the period, 'Lloyd George was delighted to turn the storm against his unruly colleagues,' such as Winston Churchill, who was Secretary of State for War at the time, and a keen advocate of British intervention against the Soviet Government.

Their intentions are less important than the fact that the Government had absolutely no choice. However much it may be argued that the Labour Movement was only acting as an accurate barometer of public opinion, the fact is that the 'Council of Action' had harnessed public opinion at a dazzling speed and had managed to translate that opinion into effective action.

Once again, as at the Shaw Inquiry, Ernest Bevin had spoken for the whole of the British working class. Having proved himself equal to the full panoply of the Law at the Shaw Inquiry, as representative of the 'Council of Action' he had now proved himself a match for one of the most brilliant and experienced statesmen of the Western world. In the process he had also shown himself to be a man of peace. It was a glorious victory.

Chapter 6

The Creation of the TGWU

At the end of 1920 world trade collapsed. It was a collapse far more rapid than any of the declines suffered since the Second World War. In particular one statistic expresses the social havoc that the recession wrought: the figure of unemployment. In a period of six months between the end of December 1920 and June 1921 unemployment trebled from 691,000 to 2,171,000.* At no time in the history of our people either before or since have men and women been thrown out of work at such a phenomenal rate.

In this atmosphere a hastening recession Lloyd George chose to hand back the mines to their owners. With demand and prices falling fast the owners gave notice that the new rates of pay would be infinitely lower (in South Wales, the worst case, the cut in pay was to range from 40% to 49%,) and that there would be no further national negotiations, only district negotiations.

Recognising that what the mineowners sought to apply to the miners could even more easily apply to them, the transport workers and the railwaymen offered support through the 'Triple Alliance' which until then had proved so successful. In the view of many, an historic contest was about to begin.

After a number of abortive negotiations, the three executives of the 'Triple Alliance' met for the last time on 13 April and agreed to call out their members at 10 p.m. on Friday 15 April. But on the evening of 14 April, a member of the miners' executive intimated that the miners would be prepared to negotiate a deal so long as it provided district minimums and a cost of living guarantee. It appeared a life-line; a sound reason to call off the strike. However by one vote the miners'

* Cf. Nov '79 1.3m and Nov '80 2.1m.

executive disowned the suggestion made by their Secretary and instead Herbert Smith, the Miners' President, issued the instruction: 'Get on t'field. That's t'place.'

Once the news of this split reached Unity House, the NUR headquarters, where the railwaymen and transport workers' executives were in session, their response was unequivocal. With such slender support amongst the miners, they were not prepared to add theirs. By 37 to 3 they decided to withdraw their strike notices. Bevin voted with the majority.

In a firework party of recriminations and accusations of treachery, this decision split the Alliance into fragments. Commenting on what was to become known as 'Black Friday,' the *Daily Herald* wrote: 'Yesterday was the heaviest defeat that has befallen the Labour Movement within the memory of man. It is no use trying to minimise it. It is no use pretending that it is other than it is. . . . They have not stood together and they have reaped the reward.'

To Bevin the defeat was a severe setback. He had been as eager as any union leader to see the Alliance work. For that reason in the Winter of 1920 he had asked for a special meeting with the other executives to overhaul the Constitution. The miners had stalled and now the Alliance was in ribbons at the beginning of the worst recession the world had ever seen. Due to the slump and the disarray of the unions, the year 1921 saw the largest single drop in trade union membership ever recorded: an exodus of 1¾ million members.

In his endeavours to bring a much more closely knit and more permanent form of alliance together through the amalgamation of all transport unions, nothing could have done more to convince Bevin of the wisdom of his next move than this stinging defeat. To Bevin the collapse of the 'Triple Alliance' was like a trumpet call to amalgamate as quickly and as completely as the unions concerned would allow.

On 1 January 1922 Bevin realised his dream of amalgamation: the Transport and General Workers' Union was born. Bevin was its architect and surveyor; its builders were the rank and file of 14 unions.

The story of its creation is the story of one man's determination to create a structure strong enough to match the most powerful employer or combination of employers or government; that is to say put the weakest section of society permanently on equal terms with any authority that might oppress it.

Bevin had seen the Triple Alliance fail and the Transport Workers' Federation creak. He feared the TUC might not measure up to the test when the moment came. In his view, to preserve the autonomy of each individual union, however understandable, was an organisational weakness. To the new edifice that he had in mind Bevin wished to apply the lessons of all the successes and failures he had experienced so far so that it might withstand the most severe battering.

From the vote for amalgamation just before the First World War, Bevin knew that there was a ground swell of opinion for one big union. From the response to the success of the Shaw Inquiry, when the employees of 300 ports had acted together, he knew there was a growing awareness of the value of collective organisation on a large scale.

In his way, however, stood a formidable array of obstacles: individual unions which did not wish to lose their identity; officials who did not wish to lose their jobs; wealthy unions which did not wish to subsidise profligate unions through the pooling of funds. Every union's contributions varied; so did their benefits.

The obstacles seemed both endless and insuperable. But the success of the Shaw Inquiry had provided an unanswerable case for amalgamation, particularly since as Harry Gosling was to admit later: 'I do not think it is giving away secrets to say now that we went to that Inquiry with a very thin camouflage.... All the time we were trembling in case we had to expose the weakness of the solidarity of those whom we represented.'

Moreover the Inquiry had thrown up a man equal to the

task of uniting a large section of the Movement. It is probably no exaggeration to say that the rank and file of many unions wanted amalgamation because in Ernest Bevin they saw a man whom they wanted to lead them. They wanted the force of his individual personality harnessed to their collective strength.

The process of amalgamation took 18 months from the middle of 1920 until the last day of 1921. After a number of tentative and informal meetings at which Bevin expounded his ideas, negotiations for amalgamation first took formal shape at a meeting in Effingham House on 14 July 1920 between the Dock, Wharf, Riverside and General Workers' Union and the National Union of Dock Labourers.

The membership of these two unions numbered 190,000. If these two rival unions could agree, they had the basis for amalgamation. But Bevin also had the perspicacity to invite Harry Gosling to act as independent chairman. Independent he was not, for as the much respected President of the Transport Workers' Federation he wielded a great deal of influence with the other potential candidates, and as the General Secretary of the Amalgamated Society of Watermen, Lightermen and Bargemen he was the senior official of a potential candidate for amalgamation as well.

Agreement reached, this nucleus called for a much bigger meeting at Anderton's Hotel in Fleet Street on 18 August. Representing 13 unions, 59 delegates met. Unanimously they agreed to the principle of amalgamation and appointed a drafting committee of 13, one representative per union, to draw up a constitution. Bevin was the natural and undisputed choice of his union.

When the Committee of 13 met, they soon realised they were a far too unwieldy number to consider the intimate details of a draft constitution. So once they had approved Bevin's draft of the 'Objects, Constitution and Methods' of the new union, they appointed a sub-committee of three..

Naturally Bevin, who was to dominate the proceedings at every stage of amalgamation, was one of the three. The other two were Harry Gosling and Alf Short of the National Union of Docks, Wharves and Shipping Staffs.

In countless meetings these three applied themselves to the administrative detail essential to the success of the largest amalgamation of trade unions ever attempted. For example, they agreed that the new union should take over all the officers of the existing unions without loss of pay. For example, they proposed that existing members could continue to pay their old rate of contributions and receive their old benefits or pay the new rates and receive the new benefits, whichever they preferred. They were well aware that rigidity in such delicate matters could undermine the foundations of their new creation.

At every stage Bevin led the small committee down avenues of his own choosing. But one aspect of the new union which cannot be attributed to him is its title. Bevin proposed 'Inland Transport Union'. Possibly because the Committee had added a trade group entitled 'Aerial Transport' into the list of occupations to be covered, the other members of the Committee preferred the Transport and General Workers' Union.

The author of this title was the Irishman James Larkin, who had founded a union of that name in Ireland before the First World War. Described by a contemporary as 'a crater through which volcanic rumblings emerged,' Larkin conducted the Irish T & G on a rampage of industrial action through Dublin in 1913, a rampage which culminated in a massive lock-out of all the T & G members in the city.

The Draft Constitution complete, the delegates assembled once again at Anderton's Hotel. As before, the proposals were greeted with acclaim. But the 83 delegates called for two significant amendments: that the Executive Council be wholly composed of lay* members; and that in the event of a call for a general strike a national conference be convened. Then they instructed conference to make the necessary arrangements for a ballot of the membership of all the unions involved.

For Bevin the critical moment had arrived. If he did not

* A 'lay' member is an ordinary member of the Union i.e. not a paid official.

succeed now, he would probably never have another chance. As the 550,000 ballot papers went out to the individual members, he knew that there were several unions who might vote against. He knew too that there were several strong and energetic officials who might lead their rank and file away from amalgamation.

Knowing this, he travelled all over the country from Glasgow to Plymouth, from Barry to Bermondsey, addressing huge meetings to explain the scheme. With him he brought a magic lantern and a set of coloured slides to illustrate his case.

By the end of March he could see that he was winning. Only three unions had voted against the scheme. Those that had voted for it brought with them a potential membership of 362,000. With this number already in the bag, the Committee summoned a delegate conference in May and invited nominations for the provisional officers and executive of the new union.

The delegate conference met in the Venetian Rooms of the St Pancras Station Hotel on 11 May 1921. Bevin reported the success of the countrywide vote. Then the delegate vote for officers of the union began. They elected Gosling provisional President, and Bevin provisional General Secretary. They agreed that the new union should come into existence on 1 January 1922. Its offices were to be in Central Buildings, Westminster; cheek by jowl with Government.

The seven month period of transition was uncomfortable. The unions lost membership and many of the 250 officials complained to Bevin that they did not know what to do. Particularly because of the deepening recession, it was far from a honeymoon period, more like a turbulent engagement. But there had to be an interval, while a committee drew up rules and every union was given a chance to consider them.

Throughout this painful process Bevin had one overriding aim: to devise a constitution which would concentrate command of the new organisation in the hands of an effective executive while at the same time providing a large degree of autonomy for each group. What he wanted was power to lead without stultifying the enterprise or infringing the legitimate rights of individual groups.

To achieve these apparently contradictory aims, Bevin fashioned a number of self-regulating devices, which created a balance of power and which remain the hallmark of the union today. So he proposed a dual system of representation which would interlock at several levels. To retain some of the identity of the old unions he proposed that each trade should be represented both regionally and nationally by a trade group. At the same time he urged that these trade representatives be merged with other trades within an area committee regionally, and within the Executive Council nationally.

In the method of operation he effected another interesting division of responsibility. Each trade group was to be responsible for drawing up its own programme, forming its own claims and carrying out its own negotiations. To balance that freedom, though, Bevin invested in the Executive Council the control of finance, the authority to call for strike action, and the right to decide the general policy of the union. Unity, with the minimum loss of freedom, was his twofold aim.

His proposal for the recruitment of staff, a vital area of control, was ingenious. He recommended appointment as the appropriate means of selecting officials; on the face of it a quite undemocratic way of approaching the matter. But he balanced this proposal with the suggestion that all officials should be answerable to a lay committee of working trade unionists elected by the rank and file.

There were to be two exceptions to the principle of appointment, however: the posts of General Secretary and Financial Secretary.* The General Secretary could only be elected through a ballot of the whole membership. But once elected he held tenure of office until retirement.

Against dictatorship and tyranny of any sort, there were to

* The TGWU no longer elect their Financial Secretary.

54

be two essential safeguards: the General Executive Council and the Appeals Committee. Elected and composed wholly of lay members, the General Council was effectively the parliament of the Union, and the General Secretary was to be answerable to the Council in much the same way as the Prime Minister is answerable to the House of Commons. But the ultimate safeguard was the Appeals Committee, elected annually by the full delegate conference to hear appeals lodged against the decisions of the Executive.

These were the basic bricks of the great industrial edifice that Bevin was constructing in those months leading up to amalgamation. However painful the process, the care with which he had undertaken the task yielded a rich harvest on 27 September when the delegates met for the last time as separate unions. During the three-day Conference they considered 2,000 amendments and completed a 70-page agenda without coming to blows.

Bevin had good reason to be well pleased with the Conference. On nearly every issue Conference endorsed his recommendations. On only one major issue did they dissent: they wanted an annual conference and not a biennial one, as Bevin had suggested. On that issue Bevin was temporarily on the losing side.

Only one obstacle remained in Bevin's way: Ben Tillett, the silvery-tongued hero of the Great Dock Strike, the boy who ran away from home to join a circus and went on to become the General Secretary of the Dock, Wharf, Riverside and General Workers' Union. What was to become of Tillett?

In recognition of past services Tillett expected to be made President of the new Union for life. From his protégé, Bevin, he expected support. But Bevin had no intention of giving that support. In his view, the amalgamation was going to prove far too fragile to sustain the election of two individuals from the same union to the two most prestigious posts. Although a subordinate in Tillett's union, Bevin told Tillett to stand down to the election for the post of President. Very reluctantly Tillett complied.

From that day the removal of Tillett has always been cited as an example of Bevin's ruthlessness. It is hardly a fair accusation. Tillett played no part in the amalgamation. Bevin secured him appointment as International and Political Secretary at his old salary. He allowed Tillett to write a special explanation to the voters to state why he was not standing. He never attempted to oust him from the General Council of the TUC and he supported the proposal to allow Tillett to remain in office until he was 70 years old. On occasions Bevin was certainly ruthless, but less so with Tillett. He treated Tillett far more gently than a number of his other opponents.

The creation of the Transport and General Workers' Union was the foundation stone of Bevin's career. Everything that happened before the formation of the Union led *to* it. Everything that developed after it led *from* it.

His lack of a trained skill, his political education and revolutionary conviction, his Christian background, his ability to lead, his audaciousness and his width of vision led *to* its creation. The role he played within the TUC, his appointment as Minister of Labour and National Service in 1940, and his appointment as Foreign Secretary developed *from* it.

As Francis Williams says in his book: 'Bevin was an organiser in the sense that some men are writers or artists. He found in organisation his mode of self-expression: it was a primary tool of his personality.... To understand him it is necessary to understand it. For to him it was much more than a practical machine for doing certain things; it was an extension of his personality.'

Chapter 7

'Red Friday'

The recession bit deep. For the next two years trade unions seldom put in a claim. It was always the employers who were seeking meetings: to demand reductions in wages, increases in working hours and withdrawals of the benefits won in better times.

In these threatening circumstances the new Union was on the defensive. To retain its unity, Bevin spelt out its priorities: the preservation of national negotiations, the maintenance of their standard of living, and the retention of their conditions.

Time and again Bevin was to negotiate a reduction in pay over this period, doing his best to restrict the reduction to the corresponding fall in the cost of living. But over the worsening of conditions he was adamant. At a special delegate conference in March 1922 he explained his reasoning: 'To get the eight-hour day established it took 30 years of effort. You can recover wages – the money side is not so difficult. When trade revives, then is the chance to recover wages. But it is the conditions. Conditions take years to recover ... and you must fight to keep them.'

At the end of 1923 the tide turned. The improvement coincided with the advent of the First Labour Government under Ramsay MacDonald. As one of the principal contributors to Labour victory, the public expected the Union Movement to moderate their claims. But Bevin saw no case for this, particularly since the Labour administration was a minority government, in office rather than in government, and wholly dependent upon the Liberals for support. Having had to restrain his members in the hour of their weakness, he was not going to hold them back in the noon-tide of their opportunity. That would have only destroyed the amalgamation.

So early in 1924 Bevin vigorously supported a national dock strike and then a London tram strike.* Both clawed back pay lost in the recession. Both helped cement the amalgamation and prove the advantage of a large union, particularly the tram strike during which 20,000 busmen came out in sympathy.

Now the Press cast Bevin in the role of tyrant. He was 'Boss Bevin', the dictator. During the tramway dispute *The Athenaeum*, for example, commented: 'We can recall no case in which a strike leader has assumed so truculent and irresponsible an attitude as Mr Bevin.'

Harking back to his Bristol days, unpopularity did not disturb Bevin at all. Early in 1925 at a delegate conference he justified the line he had taken and enunciated a principle dear to his heart: 'Whatever the defeats or gains on the political side may be, the immovable defence of the workman is always the trade unions and, whilst at all times using our efforts to capture the Government of the country, we must not for one moment slacken our efforts to strengthen the industrial machine.'

The improvement in the economy did not continue. After the fall of the Labour Government, the new Conservative Government under Stanley Baldwin, decided to return to the Gold Standard at the pre-war parity of the pound. At a stroke this put up the price of British exports by 10%. By the standards of the time this was a colossal price increase and had the effect of crippling a large section of British industry.

The coal industry in particular was to suffer a double blow. Not only did they lose export markets through this increase in price, but also through the withdrawal of the French troops from the Ruhr, which the French had occupied in a vain attempt to exact war reparations from the Germans.

* Ramsay MacDonald personally appealed to Bevin to call off the tram strike for the sake of the Labour Government. Bevin refused and bad relations between MacDonald and Bevin stemmed from this incident.

While the French were there, German coal production slumped and German industry depended in large part on British coal. When the French left, German coal production improved and orders for British coal ceased.

The effect of these two events caused another round of deflation, and hard on the heels of the price falls, there followed another round of wage cuts. Once again in the front line of the battle were the miners. From the miners, the owners wanted a reduction in wages, an increase in hours and the end of national agreements. It was a familiar story.

By themselves, there was not a chance of the miners warding off the employers' attack. But on this occasion it was even more obvious than in 1920 that what was about to happen to the miners would inevitably happen to the rest of the Trade Union Movement. According to the miners, Stanley Baldwin had said more than once: 'All the workers of this country have got to take reductions in wages to help put industry on its feet.'

But the spectre of the wrecked 'Triple Alliance' haunted the Movement and no union was as keen to enter into a pact as they had been before. Yet the 1924 TUC at Hull had moved in that direction. Then Conference had given the General Council the right to intervene in a dispute which indirectly affected others and, if necessary, 'organise all such moral and material support as the circumstances may appear to justify'.

Potentially the notice that the owners had given the miners was likely to lead to such a dispute and the Movement looked to Bevin to concentrate his organisational talents on the construction of a new industrial alliance. This time the idea was to create a fighting force far larger than the 'Triple Alliance', one which included several engineering unions such as the Electrical Trades Union. Bevin told them that they should not even talk about an alliance until they had agreed a constitution.

This time there was to be no strike until all the members knew all the circumstances and facts of the dispute involved.

Moreover, once strike action was sanctioned, the Executive of the new Alliance was to be responsible for conducting the action. At the Constitutional Conference in July 1925 Bevin spelt out the need for every constituent union to accept the loss of autonomy or scrap the idea of an alliance altogether. The Conference unanimously accepted the Constitution which was almost wholly Bevin's work. Afterwards Herbert Smith told the miners: 'Through the Industrial Alliance we got such an atmosphere created in the trade union world as we have not had before.'

With the General Council of the TUC declaring for the miners, with a new Industrial Alliance agreed in principle, with an undertaking from the International Transport Workers to 'black' all movement of coal to Britain, with an undertaking from the International Miners' Federation not to supply any coal, and an embargo threatened from the same date by the railwaymen and the transport workers, the Government had no alternative but to intervene. The situation was already out of hand.

The Government's intervention culminated in capitulation. After asking the miners what they could give in return for a concession and receiving the answer, 'Nowt', the Government offered to underwrite the present earnings of the miners for nine months from 31 July 1925, and appointed a commission of inquiry to come up with a solution during this period of grace.

Joyfully, the *Daily Herald* proclaimed the victory 'Red Friday'. It all seemed too easy. They had stood together and won. Bevin's stock rose to a new peak and nearly all the leaders in the Trade Union Movement thought they had found a formula which could be invoked to great advantage on future occasions.

In September 1925 the TUC elected Bevin a member of the General Council for the first time. From those whose opinion he most valued, it was a suitable accolade at a moment of triumph. For those outside the movement, though, his elec-

tion to the General Council must have come as a surprise –
that the best known and most powerful individual in the
Movement was not a member of its most prestigious body
already.

Chapter 8

General Strike

Had Bevin master-minded the strategy of the TUC in the miners' dispute, its outcome would most probably have been quite different. First of all, it is unlikely that the General Strike would have occurred. Secondly, if negotiations had failed, it is inconceivable that an industrial force led by Bevin would have suffered as complete a defeat as the unions did.

Even so in those aspects of the conflict in which the unions excelled, Bevin's contribution was massive. More than any other member of the General Council he managed to persuade nearly every trade union to give up their right to run their own affairs and subjugate themselves to the direction of the TUC for the duration of the dispute. Then in charge of organisation at the TUC's headquarters in Eccleston Square he overcame magnificently the complete lack of preparation for the conflict.

However, both during the run up to the Strike and during the Strike itself, the part that Bevin played was always a subsidiary one. At no point was he in charge to the extent that he was at the Dockers' Inquiry or at the meeting with Lloyd George on behalf of the 'Council of Action'.

The timing of his arrival on the TUC General Council determined his subsidiary role. By becoming a member as late as September 1925 he had denied himself the opportunity to dominate its proceedings and committees in time to become its natural leader at this moment of peril.

Even before Bevin's election to the General Council the TUC had set up a special industrial committee to guide TUC policy over the mining dispute. This was the body to which the Movement looked for direction and leadership, but there was never any question of Bevin being one of its members.

Besides, Ben Tillett already represented the Transport Workers on the Committee.

In fact Bevin had probably put his faith in the emergence of the 'Industrial Alliance' as the most effective engine of defence in the event of any breakdown in negotiations between miners, owners and Government with himself as its supreme commander. He had probably not envisaged the TUC taking over.

But in the Winter of 1925 the 'Industrial Alliance', which looked so potent a force at the time of 'Red Friday', crumbled. Fearful of losing their autonomy the railwaymen had withdrawn and from the votes of other unions it was clear that support for the Alliance was only lukewarm.

So without this new flagship, without membership of the key committee, and in spite of his public prominence and proven ability, Bevin was on the sidelines in the run up to the General Strike. However frustrating, Bevin knew in the early stages that there was nothing he could do about it.

Meanwhile the Industrial Committee was in a state of paralysis. In their minds a General Strike was unthinkable. The recession was biting deeper, membership was falling and they feared a military response to a mass stoppage.

Only Walter Citrine, Secretary to the Committee and acting General Secretary to the TUC made any real attempt to think through the consequences of a failure to find a solution to the mining problem. In an extraordinarily effective 'Memorandum on the Impending Crisis', the ex-electrician from Merseyside urged preparation on a multiplicity of fronts for the clash he feared. But with the prospect of the Samuel Report* looming, the other members of the Committee managed to silence him and his report never reached the General Council.

Indeed the country waited with bated breath for the Report of the Royal Commission of Inquiry. It was as if the whole

* This was the Royal Commission of Inquiry set up by the Government at the time of 'Red Friday' and headed by Sir Herbert Samuel, former Liberal Home Secretary.

country sensed that its future depended upon its findings (and it sold no less than 100,000 copies, the highest number of copies ever sold of any official publication at the time).

Nobody set greater store by its recommendations than the TUC. In spite of the fact that not one single trade unionist, not one single miner, not one single member of the Labour Party was a member of the Commission, the TUC deferred all forms of preparation to await its outcome. In contrast, the Government had already set up the Organisation for the Maintenance of Supplies to keep essential services running in the event of a major industrial conflict.

Yet when the Commission published its report on 10 March 1926, the bulk of its recommendations were more favourable to the miners than many had expected. It recommended no reduction in hours and the preservation of national negotiations. It proposed that the Government should nationalise coal and collect royalties from the owners for the right to extract it. Above all it stressed the need for re-organisation. Only in respect of wages did it side with the owners. It recommended 'a temporary sacrifice by the men in the industry, other than the worst paid, in order to avoid the possible unemployment of hundreds of thousands of them'.

On the surface, the recommendations seemed reasonable enough and the basis for a settlement. But the miners were not prepared, under any circumstances, to return to the negotiating table with the owners with the reduction of wages as a pre-condition. So they rejected the Report and made the slogan 'Not a minute on the day, not a penny off the pay', their battle-cry, rendering negotiations practically impossible.

Bevin felt that the Report made a great deal of sense. 'I must confess that the Report had a distinct fascination for me,' he wrote afterwards. 'I felt that if minds were applied with the right determination to give effect to it, what with re-construction, re-grouping and the introduction of a new

64

element in the management of the industry, there would in the end be produced a higher wage standard.' But whatever his view he remained in the shadows.

By 21 April he felt so ill-informed and so concerned about what might happen that he got in touch with A. J. Cook, the fiery Secretary of the Miners' Federation to find out what was going on.* What he heard from Cook disturbed him so much that he decided there and then to construct a draft of a scheme based on the Royal Commission's recommendations.

At the same time he set to work on the all-too-familiar question of how the Union Movement was to harness its power, if negotiations broke down. As before what Bevin wanted to do was to persuade all the unions involved to hand over full control to a central command; in this case to the General Council of the TUC.

Three days before the lock-out was due to begin, the TUC met to discuss a scheme of action for the first time; so unwilling had they been before to prepare for what many people feared was about to happen. To draw up the details they appointed a 'ways and means' sub-committee. As a member of this committee, Bevin became directly involved, also for the first time.

Now after so many weeks of inertia based on the expectation of a settlement, events were to move fast. On 29 April the General Council summoned a meeting of all unions affiliated to the TUC at the Memorial Hall Farringdon Street, where the Labour Party had been born 26 years before.

There, before the executive committees of 141 unions, Bevin had his first chance of influencing the direction of events. Seconding the key motion, he spelt out the implications of handing over the negotiations to the TUC:

'You are moving to an extraordinary position. In 24 hours from now, you may have to cease being separate unions. For

---

* This was the day on which the Duchess of York (The Queen Mother) gave birth to the present Queen at 17 Bruton Street, barely a mile from where Bevin was telephoning.

65

this purpose, you will have to become one big union with no autonomy. [Cheers]. The miners will have to throw in their lot and come into the course of the general movement and the general movement will have to take responsibility for seeing it through.'

On behalf of the General Council Bevin asked all the 828 delegates to remain in London while negotiations between Government, owners, miners and the TUC took place. 'You are to be our constituent assembly, an assembly where we will place the facts and the figures and the proposals and the problems that have to be submitted for calm judgement and at the end take your instructions.'

Throughout Friday 30 April the delegates whiled away their time in the smoke-filled Memorial Hall, singing hymns ('Lead, Kindly Light' was the most popular) and music hall songs, playing cards and anxiously discussing what might be happening to the various teams of negotiators dotted around London.

There was deadlock. One set of proposals after another was turned down by one side or another. Friday came and went. On Saturday the owners duly locked out the miners and the Government declared a 'state of emergency'. Still the four parties talked.

With one million miners now on the streets, the moment of truth had come for the rest of the Movement. Would the TUC stand by the miners? For the miners the moment of truth had also arrived. Would the Miners' Federation give up its precious autonomy?

Just after noon on that fateful Saturday the Conference resumed. In an atmosphere of tension and emotion the TUC asked the unions to hand over their powers to the General Council and carry out its instructions 'both regarding the conduct of the dispute and financial assistance'. All the unions of any size, representing over $3\frac{1}{2}$ million members, committed themselves unreservedly to the leadership of the TUC. Only the Seamen's Union refused to support the call.

At the eleventh hour Bevin's dream of a unified command

had come true. Under the authority of the TUC all the unions concerned issued instructions, put together by Bevin, to their members in specified trades to stop work from midnight on 3 May, 'if a settlement had not been found'.

But, in spite of the fact that Bevin drew up the plans for the Strike, he still believed, possibly more strongly than any other member of the General Council, that it was possible to find a solution by negotiation before the instructions took effect. So late on Sunday night, while the Negotiating Committee were with the Prime Minister and his team at No. 10 Downing Street, and the rest of the General Council were closeted with the miners' negotiating committee at No. 11 Downing Street, Bevin hammered out a new formula.

Bevin's basic formula centred round a national mining board composed of representatives of the Government, miners, owners and nominees of both. The Board was to be responsible for both implementing the recommendations of the Samuel Report and adjusting wages and conditions, if necessary. In the meantime, he looked to the Government for a temporary extension of the subsidy so that the wages and hours of the miners could remain unaltered.

What Bevin was trying to do was to bring forward re-organisation and put back the prospect of a reduction in wages or an increase in hours. His aim was to give the efficiencies that came from re-organisation sufficient time to obviate the need for any adjustments. It was an ingenious proposal and found much favour.

By one o'clock in the morning Bevin had seven clauses down on paper and the General Council, including the Negotiating Committee who had temporarily returned, were on the point of agreement with the three miners' representatives, when there came a knock on the door. The Prime Minister wanted the TUC Negotiating Committee to return immediately.

Standing by himself, Baldwin announced in grave tones: 'Since we were here an hour ago, an incident has happened which the British Cabinet takes such a serious view upon that they have instructed me to break off negotiations.'

The incident that he referred to was the refusal of the printers on the *Daily Mail* to print that morning's paper. They had taken exception to the leading article entitled 'For King and Country', which branded all trade unionists as traitors. In the view of the Cabinet, interference with the freedom of the Press made further negotiations impossible.

From this moment the General Strike was inevitable. But in his determination to bring the matter to a satisfactory conclusion at the earliest possible opportunity, Bevin did not let go. Before leaving Downing Street, all the trade unionists present worked on the draft for another hour. Then the following morning with Pugh and Citrine, Bevin met the three miners' leaders again in his own office at Central Buildings, Westminster. Together they reached full agreement on his draft.

This was a triumph. For the first time someone had persuaded the firebrand Cook and the dour, unyielding Yorkshire prize-fighter Herbert Smith to accept that their members might ultimately have to accept a reduction in pay. Bevin had achieved this coup through a reference to the maintenance of 'a' national minimum, which clearly implied the possibility of a reduction.

Although subsequently the full Miners' Executive rejected the use of the word 'a' to describe their minimum wage (by 12 votes to 6) and wanted the word 'the' put in its place, this was a major breakthrough. Unanimously the General Council accepted Bevin's proposals, and had the Government given its support it is difficult to believe that the miners' leaders would have been unable to persuade the rest of their Executive to vote for its acceptance.

Of course there is a question mark over whether the Government would have accepted Bevin's proposals. For reasons which have never become clear Ramsay MacDonald refused to put them to the House of Commons that afternoon.

But Bevin had few doubts. In the debate on the repeal

of the Trades Disputes Act 20 years later, referring to Baldwin's decision to break off negotiations, he said: 'We were within five minutes of a settlement.'

Now with his own organisation at the forefront of the battle and rock solid in their support of his organisation's call, Britain was to wake up on 4 May to find the whole of its transport system at a standstill. No man had brought the Movement closer to a settlement. Now no man was to do more to make the Strike work.

The response to the strike call amazed both Government and trade unions alike. Although it was only a sympathetic strike, one from which the strikers could derive no direct benefit, there was no area of revolt. In London on the first day, not one of the General Omnibus Company's 3,300 buses moved. In the docks, a particularly vulnerable area, only 40 out of 14,000 turned up for work. From the North, the Government proudly announced, one train is 'being run daily, which stops at every station!'

Meanwhile at 32 Eccleston Square, the TUC offices and strike headquarters, there was chaos. There were not enough meeting rooms. There were not enough telephones. There was no clear procedure for processing inquiries or issuing rulings.

After one day of this bedlam, in the words of Citrine: 'Bevin rose in the Council, with determination on his face, and offered to sacrifice himself on the altar of duty. He was willing to undertake the whole administration of the Strike, and thus relieve the anxieties of his colleagues.'

A naked bid for power! But the General Council avoided the need to appoint a commander-in-chief by setting up a small strike organisation committee, with Bevin included. From that moment Bevin became the field commander and applied his immense organisational powers to the success of the Strike.

For staff he drew liberally not only from the TUC but also from the Labour Party and other unions whose offices were near. Carefully defining each committee's responsibility, he gradually eliminated the confusion. He moved the Transport Committee, responsible for the issue of transport and food permits, to the Railwaymen's headquarters at Euston; a public services committee was to decide upon the distribution of electricity and gas; an intelligence committee was to collate reports about what was happening for the use of the General Council. Within hours Bevin had set up a courier service of dispatch riders to carry instructions and bring back information.

It was a prodigious feat of organisation and it worked. Throughout the nine days, the numbers on strike gradually increased. At the beginning of the second week the engineering and shipyard workers joined the Strike just as enthusiastically as the first wave. At no point was there ever a sign of a split in the ranks. Moreover 24 hours after the call to return to work the number of men on strike had actually increased by 100,000.

But whereas in the field unity and confidence reigned, amongst the General Council there was despondency and fear. Although reports from the regions were a constant source of encouragement to the General Council, in the long term they foresaw a complete impasse, the use of force and ultimate defeat. Nobody on the General Council believed that by prolonging the Strike they would get better terms for the miners and so, while their support held and before there was bloodshed, they resolved to settle as hastily as they could; too hastily as it turned out.

As always the obstacle in their way was the intransigence of the miners. Nobody could persuade the miners to compromise or even see the danger of their position without the support of the rest of the Movement; not even Sir Herbert Samuel who had returned from a writing holiday in Italy to try and break the deadlock. Chained to the Operations Room in Eccleston Square, Bevin was not involved in these endless discussions.

Yet when the General Council decided to call off the Strike it was Bevin they called upon, and not the Negotiating

Committee, to go and explain their decision to the miners and try to persuade them for the last time to 'make common cause' with the rest of the Movement. According to the miners' record, Bevin appealed to them to go back with the other unions: 'That would show a spirit of solidarity unequalled in this or any other country and he believed the terms offered would help the miners ultimately if not immediately.'

But the miners would not budge. They felt that negotiations had taken place behind their back and repeated that there was nothing to negotiate about, as they were not going to accept any change in conditions. So Bevin left empty-handed with the Movement split asunder, knowing that in a few minutes time the Negotiating Committee was due at 10 Downing Street to inform the Prime Minister that the General Council had decided to call off the Strike.

For the first time Bevin accompanied the Negotiating Committee. Whether he was invited to do so, we do not know. What we do know is that after seeing the miners, Bevin quickly took a taxi cab and joined the Committee in Downing Street. We know because Bevin has left a valuable record of that day, which other eye witness accounts confirm.

After being let in, Sir Horace Wilson, Permanent Secretary to the Minister of Labour, told them the Prime Minister would not see them unless they could confirm that the Strike was to be called off. Bevin records: 'I said at the back, "For Christ's sake let's call it on again if this is the position".' For the Negotiating Committee Jimmy Thomas acknowledged that that was what they had come to tell the Prime Minister. It was a humiliating start.

Worse was to come. When the spokesman from the Negotiating Committee explained the General Council's position, they made no reference to the withdrawal of the mineowners lock-out notices, or the need for the Government's public acceptance of the Samuel memorandum, or the need for an undertaking guaranteeing no victimisation.

The spokesman simply asked for the Prime Minister's assistance, which he gladly gave.

Again Bevin intervened. From the Prime Minister he wanted to know the answer to two questions: whether he was 'prepared to make a general request, as head of the Government, that ready facilities for re-instatement and that kind of thing shall be given forthwith'; and whether the Prime Minister was 'going to call the parties together in order to effect a just settlement'?

Baldwin replied: '... I think you may trust me to consider what has been said with a view to seeing how best we can get the country quickly back into the condition in which we all want to see it.'

Then the Prime Minister tried to terminate the meeting. But Bevin held on: 'I am a little persistent. I do not want to take up your time, but shall we be meeting on these two points soon?' To which Baldwin replied: 'I cannot say that Mr Bevin. I think it may be that, whatever decision I come to, the House of Commons may be the best place in which to say it.'

It was unconditional surrender and back at Eccleston Square, Bevin remarked bitterly: 'Something has happened and the best way to describe today, if we are not quick, is that we have committed suicide. Thousands of members will be victimised as the result of this day's work.'

It was a black day, blacker than 'Black Friday', and the unions paid a heavy price. They lost a third of their funds and over the next 18 months they lost ½ million members. On the railways, in particular, they had to fight a number of fierce battles to keep their members in their old jobs. In the TGWU, Bevin launched a counter-attack and by the end of May he was able to report that out of the 353,000 members who had struck, the Union had failed to get re-instatement for less than 1,500.

Of course the Government rejoiced in their victory, but morally it was far from complete. The rank and file had stood loyally together. In spite of the presence of troops not one trade unionist had fired a shot. In a simple, dignified way they had shown that in their thousands (at the height of the dispute 2 million were on strike and one million locked out) they were prepared to stand by their fellow men regardless of the consequences and no Government has, or ever will, forget that.

Of the leaders only Bevin enhanced his reputation. 'The big man of the strike, if anyone was entitled to that epithet, was Ernest Bevin,' wrote the *Yorkshire Post*. 'It was his quick brain and natural genius for organisation that saved the Strike from being a complete fiasco.' The *Sunday Express* went further: 'He alone took a comprehensive view. He made up his mind while others drifted. He acted while others talked – not for the first time.'

To the miners, everything that Bevin most feared occurred: their wages were cut, their hours lengthened and their national agreements dismantled. They were neither nationalised, nor re-organised. From this failure to reconcile the conflicting strands in society, the whole country suffered. The mining industry did not become efficient until the Second World War and the loss in exports alone amounted in value to thousands of millions of pounds, and it would appear that the outcome might have been different, if Bevin had been in charge at the TUC.

Chapter 9

New Horizons

The General Strike marked a watershed in the history of Britain. Before it occurred, there was a feeling that the conflicts of interest that existed between capital and labour had to be worked out in direct industrial struggle. After, there was an increasing desire on all sides to see less destructive means used to achieve political and industrial ends.

Although Bevin hammered away at increasing the size of the TGWU through amalgamation (the accession of the 100,000-strong Workers' Union in 1929 was a special triumph), he never tried to resurrect the Industrial Alliance. Nor did he try to create another great edifice to avenge the defeat of the Strike.

The TUC, with Walter Citrine now confirmed as General Secretary, was moving in the same direction. Under his meticulous guidance the TUC wanted more influence in the corridors of power; more say for their members in the running of the economy. They no longer sought to exploit or build up the tremendous firepower that the solidarity of the trade unions in the General Strike had proved was available.

So when Sir Alfred Mond, the creator of ICI, proposed joint talks with 20 of the country's most prominent industrialists, the TUC inclined towards acceptance.* Once Bevin had established that there was to be an open agenda from which no subject however controversial was to be excluded, the TUC General Council overcame the bulk of opposition. The first conference was set to take place on 12 January 1928 in the Royal Society's Rooms at Burlington House, Piccadilly.

* Mond said: 'We believe that the common interests which bind us are more powerful than the apparently divergent interests that separate.'

First results exceeded Bevin's expectations. The Employers' Group issued an amazing statement which Jim Mortimer in the 1978 Bevin Memorial Lecture said: 'Enunciates principles which even today would be regarded in some quarters as highly controversial and advanced.' The statement declared that it was 'definitely in the interests of all concerned in industry' for all working people to be members of independent trade unions. It also declared that trade unions were the 'most effective body' and 'the only body which possesses the authority' to discuss and negotiate on all questions in the entire field of industrial relations. Then it went on to repudiate, in the most categorical terms, all forms of victimisation as a result of trade union membership.

If the talks had stopped at this stage and never developed further they would have held an honourable place in the history books. But for the next two years they did go further and the parties discussed in some detail the equally controversial subjects of technology, unemployment and monetary policy.

Although these talks petered out, their effect lived on long afterwards. From the Committee considering monetary policy came a demand for a full inquiry into finance for industry which the Government set up under Lord Macmillan in 1930. From the Committee considering the re-organisation of industry came a suggestion for a National Industrial Council – the forerunner of such bodies as the National Economic Development Council.

Above all the Mond–Turner talks gave expression to the view that a considerable degree of co-operation was possible without compromise of principle. They re-established the TUC as the key representative organisation at national level and set the tone of industrial relations for the next 40 years.

At every stage Bevin had acted as chief spokesman for the TUC. At the 1928 TUC in Swansea he had warded off an attack on trade union participation from the miners' leader

Arthur Cook* with the words: 'Is the strike the only way to fight? Cannot we fight by discussion as well as by starvation? Cannot we fight by intelligence?' From now onwards, 'fighting by intelligence' was to be the hallmark of everything to which Bevin turned his hand.

On 15 May 1928 another of Bevin's dreams came true. In a simple, but moving ceremony, Transport House was declared open. The leaders of the TUC, the Labour Party and the T & G were all present. Bevin was presented with a golden key. Two plaques were unveiled: one to the Executive Council which had decided to build the offices; and the other to the workers who had constructed it.

Work had begun on the building less than two years after the creation of the Union in 1922. Well before drawing up its final plans, Bevin had captured the TUC and the Labour Party as tenants. In the summer of 1926 the Union itself had moved into the first section finished. Now its tenants, the two key arms of the Labour Movement, had come to join their landlord.

All that Bevin stood for was represented in that symbol. It was the biggest union headquarters. It was the closest to the corridors of power; within a stone's throw of the Houses of Parliament and Whitehall. It was as tall as the American Federation of Labour's headquarters in Washington (both were eight storeys high).

Before the 1929 election, Bevin urged the Labour movement to find or borrow a massive sum of money to put the *Daily Herald* on a par with the *Express* and the *Mail*. A party without a prominent national newspaper on which it could rely to put its point of view, Bevin argued, put itself at a severe disadvantage both in and out of office.

* Cook was by no means the only union leader who disapproved of union participation. There was also considerable rank and file opposition. For many it was a bad period as a result of the defeat of the General Strike.

From the Movement itself the response was poor; the unions had no wish to mortgage their future for the sake of a newspaper. But from the world of commerce came a proposition which on inspection proved irresistible. J. S. Elias, managing director of Odhams, owners of *The People*, a Sunday newspaper with a circulation of two million, sought a 'daily' companion to make use of its silent presses during the week.

So began a great partnership which was to flower to the mutual benefit of both parties. Elias provided the organisation, the money and the experience; Bevin the full support of the Labour Movement. On Monday 17 March 1929 Odhams published the first number of the new *Daily Herald*.

From a circulation of 300,000 it rose in a matter of weeks to one million, and in 1933 had the singular distinction of being the first daily newspaper in the world to reach a daily circulation of 2 million. Although many claimed that it had lost the left wing bite it enjoyed under Lansbury, nevertheless it never failed to reflect Labour's point of view.

Bevin's part in its success was in the organisation of its promotion. He enrolled 32,000 canvassers who managed to register 600,000 new readers even before the publication of the first edition. For 35 consecutive weekends Bevin himself toured the country addressing as many as three meetings a day in an effort to raise maximum support.

His interest was not entirely charitable. Although he did not receive a penny piece for his efforts, his reward lay in the indirect control that his involvement exerted over the newspaper. His contribution to its success re-inforced the 49% interest that the TUC held in the newspaper and helped keep out anybody who might consider making an attempt to replace him.

It would not have been surprising if somebody had tried a 'coup'. Five trade union directors, nominated by the TUC, represented the 49% interest. There was not a single representative from the National Executive of the Labour Party, nor from the Parliamentary Party on the Board. The political wing of the Movement had to content itself with a review of the policy of the paper at the Annual Conference 'from time to time'.

But nobody ever tried to unseat Bevin in his position as Vice-Chairman. So ultimate political control remained in the hands of the trade unions. In the 1930s it really had become 'my paper', as Bevin so often described it.

At much the same time as the new *Daily Herald* was gathering momentum, Wall Street crashed and its consequences began to reverberate round Europe. The Labour Government, elected for a second term of office under MacDonald in June 1929, responded to these chill winds by setting up a committee on finance and industry. Lord Macmillan, a distinguished Scottish judge was to preside. Although antagonistic towards Bevin, Snowden, the Chancellor of the Exchequer, invited him to represent the trade unions.

Perhaps Snowden hoped that exposure to the most acute financial brains in the country would lead to a more tolerant, understanding Bevin at Government level. Whatever his motive, the opposite occurred. Bevin emerged from the Macmillan Committee horrified by the financiers' indifference to the human consequences of their policies and not at all convinced of the soundness of their case anyway.

In the early stages of the 68 days during which the Committee sat, Bevin said little. At the outset, he listened spellbound to a nine-hour analysis of the workings of the classical financial system by John Maynard Keynes, the economist. But the more he heard, the less he liked what he learnt. The guiding principle behind every financial decision seemed to be the reaction of the international money markets.

The answers of Montagu Norman, Governor of the Bank of England, distressed Bevin most. From cross-examination Norman seemed to say that there was nothing that the Bank could, or ought to do, to safeguard the workers in industry from the effects of the Bank's monetary policy. He did not even acknowledge the need to be advised on the human consequences of any policy the Bank adopted. In Norman's view these were purely political questions.

His cold responses brought to the fore the great divide which existed between the City and Industry. It did less than justice to their case for reasonable monetary controls to help revive the international confidence and the world trade on which the country depended.

Bevin's response was two fold. He signed the main report because it proposed that the currency should be managed and that it should be managed in the interests of price stability – for the first time. But with Sir Thomas Allen, the Co-operative leader, he added some reservations.

In their addendum they called for the nationalisation of the Bank of England saying: 'Private enterprise having proved totally unable to lift the country out of the morass in which it is, there seems no alternative but for the State to grapple with the problem and for large measures of State planning to be adopted.'

In a less angry and highly perceptive passage about the Gold Standard the addendum stated: 'We take the view that the Treasury and the Bank of England should be considering an alternative basis in order to minimise disturbance if such a contingency should arise.' This was an astute reference to the need to abandon the Gold Standard, which none of the experts would consider at the time of the Inquiry, but which was forced upon them only four months later.

Although nearly 50, there is no doubt that Bevin's experience on the Macmillan Committee was a formative influence on his later thinking. In the space of four years it was the third major event which was to mould his future.

From the General Strike he had seen the need to apply trade union pressure to gain more influence in the Councils of State. From the Mond-Turner talks he had recognised the need for trade unions to capture a share in the management of industry. Now from the Macmillan Committee he was to appreciate that industrial workers would always be vulnerable until the trade unions could exert some influence over the financial decisions that affected them.

All three conclusions made him more aware of the need for political power. They led him to set a higher value upon it than he had done previously. This did not mean that he wanted to change direction and enter politics, only that he sensed that the Trade Union Movement could make little further progress without acquiring political power in one form or another.

Ramsay MacDonald's Labour Government, although a minority government, should have given Bevin an immediate chance to make some political progress for the Trade Union Movement. From the beginning of 1930 Bevin had been a member of the Prime Minister's prestigious Economic Advisory Council. But the Economic Crisis of 1931, caused by a run on the pound and heavy withdrawals of gold, extinguished any hopes of radical change.

As the storm clouds gathered, Bevin spelt out his reaction to the crisis to his Executive Council: 'I am not aware at the moment as to the actual line the Government proposes to take but our attitude to the problem must be perfectly clear. We must stand firm for the equitable distribution of the new burdens over the community as a whole, based upon the capacity to pay. The City must not be saved at the expense of the working class and the poorest of our people.'

In a private session of the Macmillan Committee Bevin had made the same point: 'I have a profound objection to picking out just one class to bear the burden.' In Bevin's eyes equality of sacrifice was the minimum that MacDonald should offer for support of a stringent financial policy on the part of the Labour Movement.

Behind this spirited defence of the poorer sections of the community there lay a growing conviction that there was a better way of climbing out of the crisis: abandoning the Gold Standard, introducing temporary import controls, increasing taxes on the better-off and expanding public works.

So when MacDonald and Snowden proposed to reduce un-employment pay by 10%, increase the level of general taxation and retain the Gold Standard, there was confusion in the Labour Movement. The Labour Party, in particular, did not know what line to take. The last thing they wanted to do was to topple their Prime Minister.

To Bevin, however, the situation was crystal clear. In his view the Government's proposals were neither sound nor fair and should be fiercely opposed. He made this abundantly clear to the General Council and found Citrine of like mind.

There the matter might have rested had not the luckless MacDonald, in recognition of the special relationship that existed between the trade unions and the Labour Party, invited the General Council to Downing Street for a meeting with the Cabinet Economic Committee.

It was a fateful meeting. Not only did the TUC give the Prime Minister an unequivocal 'No' to his and Snowden's proposed ideas for handling the crisis, but they submitted a comprehensive set of their own proposals. These proposals, so several commentators suggest, persuaded Arthur Henderson, the Foreign Secretary, and the other Labour members of the Cabinet to threaten resignation, if MacDonald went through with his intentions.

It was a great clash of two economic doctrines: the classical economists, now called Monetarists, and the supporters of Keynes.* MacDonald followed the line of the bankers and classical economists, and on Sunday 23 August, having lost the support of the Labour members in his Cabinet, MacDonald resigned.

The following day the King asked MacDonald to form a non-party National Government. It lasted until October.

Without showing any real desire to enter Parliament, Bevin

---

* Although a supporter of Keynes, Bevin did not always see eye-to-eye with him. 'When I listen to Lord Keynes talking,' Bevin once said of him, 'I seem to hear those coins jingling in my pocket, but I am not sure they are really there.'

stood for Gateshead in the 1931 General Election, as a gesture of loyalty to the Labour Party. Campaigning as a Socialist who had gone out of his way to condemn the economic policy of the 'National Alliance', he suffered a crushing defeat. A Labour majority of 16,700 turned into a 'National' Liberal majority of 12,938.

Bevin, in company with all those who had remained loyal to the Labour Movement, was out in the cold. The number of Labour MP's had been reduced from 289 to 46.

In the wilderness the two arms of the Labour Movement drew closer together. On a far greater scale trade unions and Labour Party attended each other's key meetings. In the creation of the National Council of Labour they set up a really effective, joint policy-making shop. It was a time of intense debate.

Bevin's contribution was less in the development of socialist philosophy, more in the form of practical proposals, and sometimes, as Francis Williams describes, in the form of 'visionary objectives'. For example, his pamphlet *My Plan for 2,000,000 Workless* (published in 1933) amounts to a thoroughly practical programme; his broadcast 'The Britain I want to see' (transmitted in 1934), to a soaring vision.

In *My Plan for 2,000,000 Workless*, Bevin appealed for a pension increase to attract those 350,000 people aged over 65 and still working to retire; an option to retire at 60; a rise in the school leaving age to 16; and a reduction in working hours. To explore where industry might reasonably take on more people he suggested the creation of a national employment board. An academic from Cambridge University furnished the cost of Bevin's proposals in an appendix.

This was Bevin's response to the social collapse he saw on his visits to branches in places like Merthyr Tydfil which suffered an unemployment rate of 61.4% in 1933. The cost of £80 million, less the unemployment pay the Government would not have to find, seemed a reasonable price to pay for the virtual abolition of unemployment.

In contrast his broadcast, 'The Britain I want to See', was a clarion call for the country to look beyond its own immediate needs: 'I want to see Great Britain join with every nation that it can, and particularly throughout the Empire, to raise the standard of living not only of the white race, but of the great masses of coloured races throughout the world.' For international trade he called for a world currency. To secure free access to the world's raw materials he called for an international agency.

The principle on which he based all his proposals was disarmingly simple: 'I want a Britain that places humanity first.' So he asked: 'Why should our land be flooded when we have idle labour? Why should thousands of our villages be without an adequate water supply? Why should we have slums when we possess all the essentials to house our people properly?'

It was at this time that many talked of Bevin as a future Prime Minister.

Chapter 10

Labour and Re-armament

When Hitler became Chancellor of Germany in 1933, one of his first acts was to suppress the German trade unions. Overnight he arrested their leaders, occupied their offices, dissolved their organisations and abolished their right to strike.

No trade unionist, Bevin wrote in *The Record* in May 1933, could ask for a clearer illustration of what dictatorship meant. From that moment his hostility to Nazism was implacable and he appreciated sooner than any other Labour leader that the country might have to re-arm to defend itself. The destruction of the Austrian trade unions in February 1934 with artillery, tanks and machine guns sealed his determination to oppose the dictators.

It was Bevin's task and the task of the other trade union leaders such as Citrine to alert the mainly pacifist Labour Party to the voracious intentions of the 'Nazi monster'. It took them until the autumn of 1937.

The turning point in this long drawn-out debate about the surest defence against the recurrence of war came at the Labour Party Conference in Brighton at the end of 1935. Italy had just overrun Abyssinia and the question before the Conference was whether the Labour Party would endorse the need for collective action against Mussolini through the League of Nations.

The climax of the debate was the speech by George Lansbury, the 76-year-old Party Leader, a sincere Christian pacifist. Tortured by his identification with a recent commitment of the three national committees to full support of the League of Nations, Lansbury dared to speak against the Party line and tried to lure the Party away from what had been agreed.

In an unashamedly emotional appeal Lansbury concluded: 'If mine was the only voice in this Conference, I would say in the name of the faith I hold, the belief I have that God intended us to live peaceably and quietly with one another, that if some people do not allow us to do so, I am ready to stand as the early Christians did, and say: "This is our faith, this is where we stand, and, if necessary, this is where we will die".'

To a standing ovation and cheers from all sides Lansbury limped away from the rostrum, his stick supporting him. It had been a brilliant performance by a much loved, deeply-respected leader. 'Many of the women delegates were quite openly in tears,' reported Francis Williams.

But however fine the speech, its aim, in Bevin's view, was wholly and inexcusably dishonourable. So as the cheers for Lansbury died away, Bevin approached the rostrum with his powerful chin thrust forward determined to destroy any vestige of hope for a return to a pacifist policy that any delegate might have entertained.

'Let me remind the delegates,' he barked, 'that when George Lansbury says what he says today in Conference it is rather late to say it and I hope this Conference will not be influenced by either sentiment or personal attachment. I hope you will carry no resolution telling a man with a conscience like Lansbury's what he ought to do with it. If he finds that he ought to take a certain course, then his conscience should direct him as to the course he should take.'

What had enraged Bevin was Lansbury's refusal to accept the collective decision of the National Council of Labour and the Parliamentary Labour Party. In Bevin's view, Lansbury should either have resigned or kept silent as a result of the decisions of those two bodies. To parade his doubts before the whole Party after having been party to the decisions was in trade union terms unforgivable disloyalty. That is why Bevin dealt with him so harshly.

While at the same time recognising that Bevin treated Lansbury mercilessly, Francis Williams takes this explanation one step further. Williams claims that Bevin's insistence upon absolute loyalty to a collective decision was Bevin's 'greatest single contribution to the Labour Party'. It is a telling point and one of real substance.

Certainly the forcefulness with which he challenged dissent within his own union once a decision had been democratically reached would support Williams's assertion. So would Bevin's silence after the 1936 Conference, when the Party decided to vote against the Government's increase in expenditure on the Armed Services.

But whenever he felt free to speak up for re-armament, he did so forcibly. Eventually, with the help of Hugh Dalton and several trade union leaders, his pressure paid off. In July 1937 the Labour Party recognised fully that the country had to have the wherewithal to defend itself and its allies from Fascist Italy and Nazi Germany. From then onwards its policies on defence were clearer and more consistent than those of the divided Conservative Party.

By 1937 Bevin felt that his life's work was over. He was weary of the battles both inside and outside the Labour Movement. He was also ill; suffering from strain and overwork.

What he wanted to do, so he told Francis Williams, was to exercise his option to retire at 60, find a small house in the country and spend some time with his family. For far too long he felt he had neglected his wife and daughter, who by now had married a journalist from the *Daily Herald*.

Aged 56, President of the TUC and Chairman of the General Council, Bevin appeared to have reached the pinnacle of his career. There seemed no better time to intimate his intention to depart than in his presidential address. It was not that he wished to announce his retirement, rather that he wanted to prepare the ground for so doing.

His address took the form of a retrospective look at past

achievements and the re-statement of essential values. 'I am proud of this great Movement, proud of the work it has done nationally and internationally. The honour that has been bestowed upon me I value more than any honour. I would not change the loyalty of the 600,000 members of my union for all the pelf and place that society can give.'

'It is the greatest pride of my life,' he went on, in an atmosphere heavy with emotion, 'to know that in the homes of thousands of one's mates, in the branches from as far as Malta in the East to Galway in the West, there is belief in you; that they trust you and respect your integrity, and when you did me the honour of electing me to the Chair of Congress I felt it very deeply because I believe that however controversial I have been at times you have always given me credit for sincerity.'

It appeared to be the end of an era, brought forward by a notice to retire from the man who had created and built the largest union in the country, and who had given a lead and a cohesion to the whole Labour Movement in its darkest days. The career of the country lad from Winsford seemed at an end. Such harrowing events as the Coronation Bus Strike* in which he had incurred the wrath both of the public and

* The 'Coronation' Bus Strike was so called because it occurred over the period of King George VI's coronation. It began on 30 April and lasted until 28 May. The Coronation took place on 12 May and Bevin, who was President of the TUC at the time, suffered a great deal of public criticism for allowing the strike to happen, at a time when the eyes of the world were focused on the country.

In fact Bevin had little choice. The dispute concerned a demand for a reduction in hours on which the men had set their hearts because of the lack of adequate breaks within their bus schedules, and the Union's Central Bus Committee felt that negotiations, which had continued for two months, were never going to lead to a settlement. So they struck.

The decision to strike gave rise to a fierce controversy. Bevin did not want the strike, did not believe the busmen could win and assumed authority to terminate the strike over the heads of the bus section. In Bevin's view it was a deliberate attempt to undermine the Union's authority and he set out to crush those 'who are a section of his membership appeared finally to have taken a toll of his irrepressible energy.

Little did Bevin know that what lay before him was to be as daunting and taxing as anything he had ever been through. Little did he know that his presidential speech at the TUC in Norwich, was not the end of a career but merely the end of a chapter. There was to be another chapter; and then, in addition, a glorious sequel.

First there was a short interval. That is to say, by Bevin's standards, there was a quieter moment. No longer quite at the centre of things and out of the headlines, his work was the solid work of the head of a large union. It was unspectacular but valuable.

For example, as the TUC representative on a national committee he secured one week's paid holiday for 3 million workers in several industries. For the jockeys at Newmarket and the stable lads at Lambourn he secured better wages and conditions. For the lorry drivers he was instrumental in the passing of the Road Haulage Wages Act which established the principle of wage regulation in one of the most difficult industries to protect.

This solid, unexciting and detailed Union work which Bevin did needs to be emphasised. In the Flour Milling industry, for example, he set up a Joint Industrial Council as early as 1918 and, in 1937, in an atmosphere of deep and mutual respect between employers and trade union, he negotiated a cut in Hours of Work to 42 hours and a Guaranteed Wage. No other industry in the country of a similar size had such

---

trying to wreck it (the Union) and crush them once and for all, flat, finished.'

After a Court of Inquiry put forward recommendations which the Rank and File Committee rejected, the Executive Council suspended the special constitution of the Central Bus Section and ordered their own inquiry into the conduct of its members. As a result three members were expelled. Not surprisingly it remains a highly controversial episode in the Union's history.

good working conditions and between the wars the industry did not suffer a single strike.

Both employers and union were equally proud of their joint achievements in this industry. Even in the dark days of the thirties, the industry provided compensation for those who lost their jobs on account of rationalisation. In 1931 the industry also introduced a contributory pension scheme. The implementation of such arrangements in a whole industry was revolutionary. When Minister of Labour during the war, Bevin tried to apply many of the same principles and practices to those industries where work-people hardly enjoyed any protection.

Bevin and his wife, however, enjoyed one moment of real relaxation together in the latter part of 1938 and early part of 1939. For the Commonwealth Relations Conference they went by ship to Australia. In a three week voyage they sailed across the Pacific by way of Hawaii and Fiji. They returned by way of India and Africa.

Invigorated by what he saw, inspired by what he heard, rested both in body and mind, it seemed as if he was being prepared for what was to happen next. On his return, bursting with ideas and enthusiasm, he released the full range of his energies against the 'obstruction, lack of drive, absence of imagination and complacency' of the Chamberlain Government. When not railing against 'the middle class mind', he spent his time explaining to those who would listen his ideas for securing international peace in the long term.

Chapter 11

Minister of Labour and National Service

At eleven o'clock on Saturday 11 May 1940, Ernest Bevin was called to the telephone in Transport House. On the other end of the line was Clement Attlee, Leader of the Labour Party. Attlee had two questions to put to Bevin to which he required answers.

The first question was whether Bevin would support the Labour Party joining a coalition headed by somebody other than Chamberlain. To that question, Bevin replied: 'In view of the fact that you helped bring the other fellow down, if the Party did not take its share of responsibility, they would say we were great citizens but cowards.'

The second question which Attlee asked was whether Bevin would be willing to become a member of the Government himself. To that question Bevin replied: 'You have sprung it on me.' Then he added that he could only agree to serve with the agreement and support of the General Council of the TUC, the National Executive of the Labour Party and, of course, his own union.

Then Bevin asked what office he might be offered. The Ministry of Labour, Attlee replied. 'If the Ministry of Labour remains as it is now,' responded Bevin, 'purely a glorified conciliation board with the register for national service, unemployment and public assistance, it will be a waste of time.'

At this point the telephone conversation came to an end. Both Attlee and Bevin had to catch the train to Bournemouth to attend the annual Labour Party Conference. There, in the following 48 hours, Bevin consulted the three bodies concerned and won unanimous support for acceptance. Then suppressing his negotiator's inclination to demand immediately an enlarged role for the Ministry of Labour, he accepted Churchill's offer unconditionally on 13 May. But in his letter of acceptance he stressed the need to put the Ministry of Labour 'in a position to make its contribution to the actual organisation of production so as to secure the right utilisation of labour and not merely be regarded as an institution to supply the personnel'.

Bevin had acted adroitly. By insisting on the full support of the TUC and the TGWU, Bevin had put himself in an immensely strong position in two respects. The Government had to recognise the support he had. The trade unions had to recognise the commitment they had given. Had Bevin failed in the heat of the moment to consult the trade unions and accepted without their agreement, he would have severely reduced his bargaining power with both sides. To Government and trade union alike he would have appeared less representative of the Movement, merely a powerful personality whose individual ability was more important than his position and standing.

In that hour of crisis in May 1940 the temptation to accept must have been strong. For good reason Churchill did not want to wait. But Bevin insisted and in the second volume of his book on the Second World War, Churchill recognised the value of the hold-up, said it was 'worth it', and pointed out that as a result the T & G 'stuck solid for five years until we won'.

For a host of reasons Churchill's choice of Bevin was extraordinary. Bevin had never held a ministerial post, had never sat in Parliament and was not even a member of the National Executive of the Labour Party. He was known to have been ill and was on the point of retirement. Whenever he had stood in a local or parliamentary election, he had lost. He knew nothing whatever about war.

On countless occasions the two had directly opposed each other. In 1911 and 1912 Churchill had been instrumental in sending troops to try to break the strikes. In 1920 Churchill had advocated direct support of Poland in an endeavour to smash the 'Red Army'. In 1925 Churchill had brought the country back onto the Gold Standard – in Bevin's view, the original cause of the General Strike.

Finally in the General Strike the two had shaped up to each other like warring chiefs, and even three years after the event Bevin could not refer to Churchill without a tone of disgust in his voice. In an analysis of the Strike to a group of tinplate workers in Swansea in April 1929, Bevin had said: 'It will be the greatest godsend to this country if Mr Churchill is out of office for evermore.... It is not that Mr Churchill is not a brilliant man, but it is not safe to leave the destinies of millions of people in the hands of a man with an unstable mind....'

This was the background to the partnership which was about to take shape.

His first day at the Ministry of Labour was not auspicious. According to his biographer Alan Bullock, Bevin sat himself down at his new desk, called his Parliamentary Secretary Ralph Assheton, and asked: 'Well, Ralph, what do I do next?'

Taken aback by the question, Assheton respectfully explained that he could rely on his officials to put any proposals into effect provided he knew what he wanted to do. Bevin said he had plenty of ideas. To which Assheton responded, adopting the role of schoolteacher: 'Then if I were you, I would go off home and put them down on paper.'

That is what Bevin did. Next morning, like a schoolboy handing in his homework, he gave Tom Philips, his Permanent Secretary, four written sheets containing his proposals for the future.

Those four pages of scrap paper and untidy scrawl contain the seeds of all that Bevin was to do during the war as Minister of Labour and National Service. This was extraordinary. Four days before, as he packed his bags to go to Bournemouth, he did not even know of the possibility of becoming Minister of Labour and National Service. He had never aspired to the job. He had not played any part in ousting Neville Chamberlain or in bringing in Churchill to replace him. Yet within 24 hours of his appointment Bevin's powerful mind had devised a workable blueprint for the transformation of the Ministry of Labour.

What were these proposals? In structure they had a certain similarity to the construction of the Transport and General Workers' Union: centralised power modified by watchdog committee; decentralised execution effected by an army of professional officials who in their turn were answerable to a joint committee representing all interests.

First and foremost, Bevin wanted the power of decision for all manpower and labour questions, including the power to examine the use made of labour as well as the right to withdraw it, concentrated in his hands. Bevin had none of the inhibitions of Ernest Brown, the previous Minister of Labour, who only a fortnight before had reluctantly and after much indecision accepted that the Ministry should be responsible for the allocation of labour.

To arbitrate on labour priorities and at the same time leaven the absolute power of the Minister, Bevin proposed a production council to consist of the three supply Ministers, the President of the Board of Trade and Bevin himself; five in all. These five men were to have responsibility for turning strategic decisions into production programmes with the appropriate labour allocations.

Having centralised decision making, Bevin then sought to de-centralise the execution of those decisions. Through the creation of 12 Area Boards based on the same pattern as the Production Council, Bevin proposed that they should have power enough to give effect to those decisions. To investigate shortages and obstacles to these changes he proposed to recruit and train 400 labour supply inspectors.

To advise him Bevin asked for a labour supply board made up of two industrialists and two trade unionists, available if necessary, for a daily meeting. Finally, in order to

93

overcome any trade union objections to the wholesale removal of demarcation lines and restrictive practices, which
he hoped would be set aside, he proposed that Parliament
should give a formal undertaking to restore pre-war arrangements when peace came.

Six days after Bevin had first walked into the Ministry,
he was ready to present his programme of action to the
War Cabinet. On Monday 20 May, the War Cabinet accepted
almost all his proposals. They were deeply relieved that there
was somebody in charge who knew what he wanted and was
prepared to take a firm line.

Bevin's shopping list, however, contained a significant
omission. It made no reference to compulsory powers. This
was deliberate. Bevin hated compulsion, seeing in it the destruction of democracy and the negation of all that he had
stood for, and fought for, in the past.

To Bevin compulsion was the quintessence of dictatorship
and it was deliverance from dictatorship for which the
country was prepared to shed its last drop of blood. Having
seen Hitler ruthlessly deny both individual and collective
freedoms, Bevin saw no case for copying the methods against
which the country was fighting.

The cornerstone of Bevin's philosophy was what he called
'Voluntaryism'; the very antithesis of Nazism. Whereas
Nazism drew its strength from efficiencies gouged from the
withdrawal of democratic rights, 'Voluntaryism' drew its
strength from the spirit of co-operation which flowed from
their development and extension. It was based on the conviction that the 'freeborn Englishman' would make greater
sacrifices willingly rather than under compulsion.

For the trade unions such a philosophy had a dramatic im-
plication. Instead of being restricted to the back bench of the
Government machine,* Bevin intended to invite them to share
the driving seat. At every level Bevin sought their partnership.

* In the First World War the lack of real partnership between
the trade unions and the Government had given rise to the Shop
Stewards movement.

His was not a covert attempt, however, to change the balance of power. Politics aside, Bevin genuinely believed that this approach was both the only way to win the war and the only way worth winning it. Subconsciously his appointment to the Ministry of Labour was probably an acknowledgement on the part of Churchill and the Government, too, of the wisdom and rightness of this approach.

But with Europe on the point of collapse and invasion a distinct possibility, few believed that the Government could operate without any means of compulsion on which to fall back. Every party felt sure that the Government had to have some emergency powers to requisition property and direct labour.

Accordingly, on 20 May Attlee, in the absence of Churchill – who was in Paris trying to stiffen French resistance – introduced the Emergency Powers Bill into the House of Commons. Within three hours this Bill, the most drastic ever brought before a British parliament, had passed through all its stages and become an act.

Under Regulation 58A of the Act Bevin found himself empowered 'to direct any person in the United Kingdom to perform any such services' as the Minister of Labour might specify. This gave him absolute authority over the lives and activities of every civilian in the country between the ages of 14 and 64. No man in peace or war had ever had such authority conferred upon him by a British parliament.

Barely a week had passed since Churchill had become Prime Minister, and less than that since Bevin had become Minister of Labour. Yet so much had happened in those few days that it was deemed essential to hold an immediate meeting of trade union delegates. Without their co-operation Bevin was doomed.

The date chosen was 25 May; the site, Central Hall, Westminster. From the country's 150 largest unions, 2,000 delegates attended. It was the largest meeting of trade union delegates since the General Strike; in fact the largest at that time in the history of the Movement. The speaker was the same. The purpose of the meeting was the exact opposite.

In a powerful speech Bevin explained his philosophy, outlined each of the proposals he had put to the Government, and then appealed for unreserved support for the Government in whatever steps it felt necessary to take to win the war. In stirring words he concluded: 'This I am convinced of: if our Movement and our class rise with all their energy now and save the people of this country from disaster, the country will always turn with confidence to the people who saved them.'

It was an inspiring, honest, uncompromising and yet deeply understanding performance. On the one hand he flattered them: 'Machine tools today are more precious than all the banks of England.' On the other, he told them where they stood: 'I have to ask you virtually to place yourselves at the disposal of the State.' As Francis Williams says: 'It was a unique essay in industrial leadership and his own incomparable grasp of the problem.'

Then, having won support from the Movement, Bevin took his requests a stage further. He asked the delegates to go back to their places of work and tell their members the full story. In the same way as he had shared his hopes, his fears and his aims with the delegates, he wanted them to pass on what they had heard to every working man and woman with the intention of making them feel equal partners in meeting the appalling threat that confronted the country.

Even at this moment of crisis, however, Bevin never lost sight of his ultimate goal, a vision beyond the defence of democracy. In this great speech he ended with the words: 'I want, if God spares me, to play a part in trying to put international labour on terms of equality for everybody throughout the world.' It was another of Bevin's soaring dreams which took his audience beyond their immediate needs and gave them a glimpse of something worth fighting for, a promised land.

Diana Mercy Bevin, Bevin's mother, in 1881, the year of his birth.

Aged 14, Ernest Bevin four years after he started work.

In 1920, at the time of the Shaw Inquiry into dockers' wages.

AMALGAMATION

Transport and General Workers

FELLOW WORKERS:—

The great scheme of Amalgamation will be submitted to you for ballot forthwith.

The scheme has received the considered judgement of the Executives of each Union that are parties to it, and at a great Delegate Conference in London it was endorsed unanimously. (See Resolution overleaf.)

We are convinced this is the right step to take to secure the necessary power and efficiency to deal with the problems that must be solved by the Movement.

Our Unions have, in their respective sections, played a wonderful part in the past, but PROGRESS DEMANDS that existing methods shall give way to new.

CAPITAL IS WELL ORGANISED—EVERY TRADE IS INTERWOVEN AND INTERLINKED.

The great industries on the employers' side stand together ! !

Labour must do likewise. Whoever stands in the way of this great change in methods of organisation is doing a grave injustice not only to the present generations, but to the children yet unborn! The scheme allows for the creation of a GREAT and POWERFUL UNION.

> It pools its financial resources.
> It gives opportunity to create efficient methods of negotiations and handling disputes.
> It gets rid of jealousy between Unions.
> It allows for the rank and file to co-operate in port, waterway, road transport and factory.
> It gives the officials greater scope; a greater opportunity of acquiring knowledge—placing them on an equal footing with employers in dealing with your problems.
> It provides for each section to have its own National Committee.
> It allows opportunity to shape its program and policy, at the same time bringing to the assistance of any one section both the moral and financial strength of the remainder.
> It proposes to organise the whole of the workers engaged in the respective industries covered by the new Union—administrative, clerical and manual.
> It is the creation of a NEW MACHINE.
> It will ultimately not only talk of wages, but exercise greater power and control.

WE MOST EARNESTLY APPEAL TO EVERY MEMBER OF THE AMALGAMATING UNIONS TO SECURE THEIR BALLOT PAPER AND UTILISE THEIR VOTE IN ITS FAVOUR.

NOTHING CAN PREVENT IT — only two things can hinder it — namely — VESTED INTEREST and APATHY.

If vested interest stands in its way, then vested interest will be swept aside by force of events.

If, owing to apathy of the rank and file, the necessary power is not given to the Committee to go on immediately, then *the* RANK AND FILE WILL BE GUILTY of a crime against themselves, their wives and their children.

It is said it's the duty of Leaders to lead—We now give you the lead—Don't fail to respond ! !

Signed on behalf of the Delegate Conference,

HARRY GOSLING,
Chairman.

ERNEST BEVIN,
Hon. Secretary.

16

The famous "Amalgamation" call, drawn up after the conference in December 1920, to accompany a ballot of all union members. Eleven were 'for', three 'against', and by the time the amalgamation was completed, fourteen unions with 350,000 members had come together.

Bevin prepares a meal to show how little could be had from a weekly wage of £3–12–6d for a docker's family of five, as proposed by employers' witnesses at the Shaw Inquiry.

The new TGWU headquarters, Transport House, Smith Square, Westminster, was opened in 1928. Only a stone's throw from Parliament, tenants were the TUC and Labour Party.

As a matter of principle, Bevin stood (and was defeated) as parliamentary candidate at Gateshead in 1931, against Ramsay Macdonald and the National Government.

The Clarion booklet of early 1933 in which Bevin set out a bold plan to create two million jobs for the unemployed.

With Walter Citrine, TUC General Secretary, in 1937; seeing eye to eye on most policy matters, they hardly ever talked privately, despite working in the same building.

A sense of the concerns of the trades unions comes from these two front pages of Bevin's union journal, *The Record*. Top, April 1937 and below, March 1937. One for May Day, one for jobs.

The Minister of Labour and National Service spells it out to engineering trainees on a wartime factory visit in 1941.

Wartime leaders on Victory Europe day at Buckingham Palace. Churchill and Bevin stand next to H.M. King George VI.

Still visiting the shop floor, though now Foreign Secretary, at an engineering works in 1947.

Officially received in New York before a U.N. meeting, the crowds turn out on 9th November, 1946.

With Mr. Molotov, Soviet Foreign Minister, after a meeting on 11th September, 1945.

Raising the United Nations flag at Woolwich Town Hall in October 1950. He never missed a U.N. session.

With his wife 'Flo', at Southampton, after crossing from the USA on the *Queen Mary*, 4th October, 1950. His wife liked to accompany him on foreign visits.

On the way to No. 10 Downing St. in September 1950.

Epstein's sculpture.

In his history of the trade unions, *Magnificent Journey*, Francis Williams wrote:

'Thereafter there was complete co-operation between Government, employers and trade unions at every level of industrial decision. The principle of equality so long demanded by the trade unions and denied them right up to and beyond the outbreak of war was now wholly accepted. The speed and efficiency of a wartime industrial revolution which none of the totalitarian countries were able to match flowed directly from the acceptance of this principle.'

In fact the Government had not conferred equality on labour. Churchill had not invited Bevin into the Government on equal terms. The Ministry of Labour was still a minor ministry; a tool of government, rather than part of Government itself. Within a fortnight Bevin may have turned it into a mighty tool, but while still outside the War Cabinet, he played little part in the creation of policy.*

Five months later that situation changed. In October Churchill invited Bevin to join the War Cabinet. This was the moment of full recognition, of real equality, for it put the resource of labour on a par with finance, the Minister of Labour on a par with the Chancellor of the Exchequer. It was the climax of the story of the growth of trade union power which started in 1824 with the Repeal of the Combination Acts when the trade unions first won the right to bargain about wages and conditions.

In more ways than one, Bevin's appointment to the War Cabinet was a symbolic act. Britain was at her lowest ebb, suffering her darkest hour. In the space of three months Hitler had overrun five countries and had twice pushed Britain into the sea, first in Norway and then at Dunkirk. France was no longer by her side. Apart from the Commonwealth Britain stood alone, fearing and preparing for invasion. In this moment of peril Bevin's appointment to the

* Bevin was not even an MP until the end of June 1940, when he was returned unopposed for Central Wandsworth.

War Cabinet, therefore, completed a social revolution. It marked the point at which the powerful and the privileged, represented by Churchill, fully acknowledged their dependence on 'the common man', represented by Bevin, and welcomed him into full partnership for the first time.

Although a marriage born of need, it was nevertheless a marriage of free and equal partners. Bevin had not sought appointment to the War Cabinet. Churchill was not under any compulsion to include him. It was a voluntary contract freely entered into, which sealed the unity of the nation in a way that no enforced arrangement could have done. Few decisions did more to strengthen the country's will to resist and then to press forward towards victory.

At the time Bevin received the invitation he reacted with the same disarming bewilderment as he had on his first day as Minister of Labour. 'I'm very new at this game,' he told Hugh Dalton, 'and I didn't know what to say when the PM asked me last night. But I thought it would help the prestige of the Trade Union Movement and the Ministry of Labour if I went in. No one has ever put the Ministry of Labour in the forefront like this before.'

It was a vindication of all that he had protested about regarding the Government's attitude to trade unions in a message to his members in October 1939:

'The Ministers and Departments have treated labour with absolute contempt yet without the great Trade Union Movement the Forces cannot be supplied with munitions or the country with food. The principle of equality has not yet been won – equality not merely in the economic sense but in conception and in the attitude of mind of those in power.

'We do not desire to serve on any Committee or Body as an act of patronage. We represent probably the most vital factor in the State: without our people this war cannot be won, nor can the life of the country be carried on.'

Partnership, of course, brought with it direct responsibility. In the words of Winston Churchill, Bevin had become one of the 'only ones who had the right to have their heads cut off on Tower Hill if we did not win'. On the other hand, membership of the War Cabinet brought with it privileges. It gave Bevin the hallmark of true partnership, direct access to all the departments of Government; a privilege of which Bevin was to make good use.

Bevin's achievements as Minister of Labour and National Service are awe-inspiring. In summary, they amount to the mobilisation and demobilisation* of the entire nation, and a permanent change in the relationship of labour to the State.

The figures are of an order of magnitude which it is difficult to grasp. As Minister of National Service Bevin furnished the armed services with $4\frac{1}{2}$ million men and women by April 1942; in 1939 they had numbered just over 400,000. In September 1940 the Defence Committee had asked Bevin to provide the armed forces with 1.7 million more men within 16 months: he did. As Minister of Labour his task was on a similar scale. On the same date the Defence Committee asked for 859,000 more men and women for the munitions industries alone: again Bevin did so.

Of all the figures to choose from, the most dramatic concerns shell-filling. In September 1939 there were just 8,000 men and women filling shells; by December 1941 Bevin had increased that number to 144,000. Remarkably over the period of the war he achieved a net increase in the working population of 2 million, in spite of the fact that 393,000 people were killed either in action or in air raids.

No country in the history of mankind has ever mobilised itself to such extent. 'You defeated us because you made total war and we did not,' Albert Speer, Hitler's Minister for Armaments, was to say later.

Initially Bevin wielded lightly the blunt instrument of industrial conscription. In his first year of office he only issued

* A great deal of demobilisation occurred after he had left the Ministry of Labour. But Bevin worked out the system on which it was to take place and initiated the process. See below, page 106.

2,800 'orders' to individuals. By his third year, however, he had increased that number to 408,000 individual orders.

This was a complete change of approach. What had turned the advocate of free-will, of 'Voluntaryism', into the apostle of force? Answer: a major shift in public opinion. The country had come to recognise that circumstances demanded an element of compulsion that ensured fairness; that is to say, nobody could 'dodge the column'.

In Bevin's handling of compulsion lies one of the clues to his greatness. At the outset he rejected compulsion, knowing that willing workers were more productive than pressed men. Then having exhausted the available store of willingness he turned to compulsion as a last resort, knowing that the use of force would be, paradoxically, based on consent. Because of his remarkable understanding of what the country could take he managed to deploy all its energies in a way that nobody has ever achieved before or since. Compared with the opposition that laws of a similar kind provoked both in Britain during the First World War and in the United States during the Second, defiance of Bevin's instructions were minimal.

Because it was so comprehensive, his conscription of women was the most controversial aspect of his use of compulsory powers. Between 1941 and 1945 his department registered over 10 million women for national service. They included nurses up to the age of 60, cotton operatives up to the age of 55, and all women up to the age of 51.*

For his regiments of 'grannies', his parliamentary opponents attacked him scathingly. But he answered confidently: 'If we can use men and women in the factories to build up the most mighty equipment, the most powerful force, and with the sheer weight of that force shorten this war by a minute, or a day, or a month, then we shall be doing the most humane thing we can to end this holocaust.' Few dissented when it came to the vote in Parliament on conscription of women.

* Of conscription of women, Bevin said: 'Behind it is the voluntary submission to discipline of a whole people.'

There were, however, two other reasons why Bevin was markedly successful in directing people to jobs. Wherever the Ministry of Labour became involved, Bevin insisted upon the introduction of better working conditions and, where possible, fairer pay. Even in 1940 he had the nerve to raise the minimum agricultural wage to a level more closely in line with the rest of industry, remarking:

'I have told the Government that this difference between public employees and those in factories and the people in rural England must be obliterated and the old conception that agriculture is an industry of servitude must go, and go for all time. I hope not only to make a contribution to produce the necessary food but to remove a grievance which as a country lad myself has always burned in my boots.'

For the dockers he introduced a guaranteed week, more than 20 years after he had first demanded one at the Shaw Inquiry. For the ½ million people employed in hotels, restaurants, cafes, canteens, bars and boarding houses he steered the Catering Wages Bill through the Commons in 1943.

The Catering Wages Bill proposed a permanent catering commission with statutory power to fix wages and such conditions as rest periods and holidays. It was anathema to the Tory back benchers. Opposing it fiercely, they reminded the Government of their pledge not to introduce controversial measures. But the War Cabinet never wavered in their support for Bevin and the Bill became an act.

It was a significant victory for Bevin and symbolised a measure of acceptance in the country as a whole of the need for centralised control of wages and conditions. Later, the Wages Councils Bill of 1945 took this principle a stage further by elevating the Trade Boards instituted in 1909 for sweated occupations into Wages Councils with wider powers.

Such progress was dear to the trade union heart which beat so strongly in Bevin's breast. 'From time immemorial one of the leading tenets of trade unionism has been the desirability of maintaining by law the minimum Standard of

Life of the workers,' wrote the Webbs, at the turn of the century. Such acts as the Catering Wages Act were the fulfilment of this trade union goal inherited from the Craft Guilds hundreds of years before.

Progress in welfare was even more extensive. From one of his earliest meetings with the War Cabinet Bevin secured the transfer of the Factory Acts and the Factory Inspectorate from the Home Office to the Ministry of Labour. Then, through a factory and welfare division which he immediately created, he set about introducing an enormous number of improvements in working conditions which have now become a permanent part of the country's industrial way of life.

Believing that the health of the country in a long war could prove crucial, Bevin did all he could to improve the health and welfare of industry. He made an order for the appointment of full and part-time doctors. He urged employers to take on more nurses. He offered state aid to help set up canteens.

By the end of the war the figures were encouraging. The number of doctors in industry had risen from 80 to more than 1,000; the number of nurses to 7,800. He was particularly proud of the explosion of canteens he had stimulated; with the Ministry's financial support they had increased from 200 to 12,000. This meant that many of those whom he had required to leave home or travel to work would get a square meal in the middle of the day.

In a host of less dramatic ways Bevin tried to improve welfare arrangements too. For those ordered to move he set up reception centres and even some hostels. For girls journeying to a new place of work he provided escorts. For women and young people he limited overtime and strongly urged employers to apply the same limit of a maximum 60-hour week to men as well. For the disabled he established a register and made it compulsory for all firms employing more than 20 people to take on a percentage from this register. This was outstandingly successful.

In December 1943 when introducing the Disabled Persons

(Employment) Bill he proudly told the House of Commons:

'The terrible loss of skill which was involved was impressed upon me when I took office and found that nearly 200,000 people had been written off in cold blood by local committees as no good to society and a permanent charge on the Assistance Board. These men were marching up twice a week to parade their misery and their suffering and yet by measures of this kind in this war that number has now been brought down to 18,000.'

All these improvements in health and welfare were Bevin's way of responding to the 'resolute, urgent, persistent, consistent effort' which he had called for at the beginning of the War. It was his way of trying to give something back and a means of recognising that those he was moving around the country, often without explanation, were human beings first and only fighting machines second.

For all his ruthless determination to prosecute the War remorselessly, underneath so many of his ideas and policies there lay a kind of tenderness. What other quality could have inspired him to start 'Music while you work'? Refuse to suppress horse racing? Advise the Army Council that if they wanted more girls to volunteer for the ATS they ought to give them stockings which looked more like silk than dull khaki cotton?

All these improvements softened the blows of compulsion to many and created an atmosphere of progress and hope for the future, even in the darkest days of the war. It was a hope to which Bevin personally clung and did what he could to promote whenever he had the opportunity.

An early opportunity to formulate the ground of his hope came in August 1941 when President Roosevelt urged Churchill to draw up a joint declaration of principles, so that everyone everywhere should know for what sort of world the two countries were fighting. When the draft first reached the Cabinet, Bevin was the only Minister to propose an entirely new clause. It expressed in general terms what Bevin believed should be domestically the overriding post-war aim.

Bevin wanted to add: 'They support the fullest collaboration in the economic field with the object of improving labour standards, abolishing unemployment and want, securing economic advancement and social security for all people.' It was a profound and compact expression of all that Bevin stood for and a brave intervention on the part of one of the newest members of the War Cabinet.

Eventually the final version excluded the words 'abolishing unemployment and want'. But even in its emasculated form Clause 5 of the Atlantic Charter was a commitment of some value. It gave Bevin real satisfaction, since he had persuaded both British and American Governments to accept the principle of social security which paved the way for the Beveridge Report.

Indirectly Bevin was also responsible for the Beveridge Report: the biggest step of all in social reform during the War. In June 1940 Bevin had invited William Beveridge, Master of University College, Oxford and ex-Director of the London School of Economics to become head of the new Welfare Division which he proposed to set up within his Ministry.

Highly regarded and somewhat feared as Beveridge was, Bevin's permanent officials declared him impossible to work with. Faced with the possibility of a revolt, Bevin suggested to Arthur Greenwood, Minister-without-Portfolio but in the War Cabinet, that Beveridge might be asked to undertake an inquiry into social insurance and be transferred to Greenwood: Greenwood agreed.

From his lonely backwater Beveridge delivered a political blockbuster which set the political world alight. His 'Report on Social Insurance and Allied Services' was an instant best seller. Not until Lord Denning investigated the Profumo Affair did Her Majesty's Stationery Office make such sales.

Far from a simple technical report Beveridge's work was according to Bullock like 'a new declaration of human rights brought up to date for an industrial society'. A blueprint for re-construction it may have been, but politically it was also full of controversial measures. So the Coalition Government shied away from giving the Report their full support.

The furore that followed was not wholly in vain. By way of the Reconstruction Committee, the Beveridge Report lit the torch which Bevin eventually carried into the House of Commons, when he moved the adoption of the White Paper on Employment Policy. This was a stupendous development, since what Bevin was laying before the House amounted to an all-party commitment to full employment.

As this was a time when party politics were beginning to re-emerge, some members of the Labour Party were deeply suspicious of what was happening. They suspected an attempt to perpetuate the Coalition; or even worse form a 'National Government'. Nye Bevan, in particular, wanted to know how the problem of unemployment could be solved without the 'transfer of economic power'.

Bevin replied: 'The question of how you can give effect to the decision as to who will own industry is not prejudiced by this White Paper.... What we have tried to do is to devise a plan which, however you may decide the ownership of industry ..., seeks to obtain the objective (of full employment).' To an interrupter who wanted to know whether he was in favour of 'a continuous coalition', he gave a firm 'No!'.

The key promise to which the Government was proposing to bind itself is to be found in Chapter IV of the White Paper: 'The Government are prepared to accept in future the responsibility for taking action at the earliest possible stage to arrest a threatened slump.'

This meant that the Government had accepted the Keynesian principle of expanding and not contracting expenditure, of increasing consumption and not reducing it at the onset of a slump. To a greater or lesser extent it was a principle to which Governments adhered until the late 1970s.

Such a dramatic and total reversal of economic policy had never before occurred in the country's history. It was the exact opposite to the policy advocated by the bankers and pursued first by MacDonald and then by Baldwin in the 1930s.

'Today,' proclaimed Bevin triumphantly at a press conference, 'this plan just leaves the nineteenth century behind and it says in effect that instead of the human being having to fit himself into an exchange system, the exchange system has to fit into human requirements. It reverses the policy we have been following ever since the Industrial Revolution.'

Now Bevin focussed his mind on demobilisation. To help him demobilise he turned to the joint machinery which he had brought into existence at the beginning of the War to help him mobilise. Based on a formula of age and length of service together with early release for those with skills urgently needed, Bevin devised a scheme which was just as efficient and comprehensive as his schemes for the mobilisation of manpower.

By the end of the War Bevin had been a member of the Government for five years. He had mobilised the nation. He had laid the groundwork for demobilisation. In the process he had improved wages and working conditions and had established a new relationship between the Trade Union Movement and Government which was to become a permanent feature of the post-war world.

His relations with Churchill were based on mutual respect, but not intimacy. They were both kings in their own country. Churchill never invited Bevin to join the Cabinet Defence Committee. Bevin would never have let Churchill near the Production Executive; and Churchill never tried to interfere.

Occasionally they travelled together, as they did to watch part of the invading armada set sail for the Normandy landings in 1944. Otherwise outside the War Cabinet they had little contact. In his six volumes on the Second World War, Churchill makes few references to Bevin and he can't have sent more than a dozen memos to him throughout the whole war. It was a tribute to Churchill's confidence in him.

As Bevin stressed, it had been a people's war. The common people had felt compelled to fight with an intensity of purpose without parallel in the country's history. In the Councils of War Bevin had been their representative. In this respect he was not just Minister *of* Labour but Minister *for* Labour. It is not surprising, therefore, that at the end of the War Bevin emerged a legend, because what the common people – the people he represented – had done was legendary and he would not have wanted to try and distinguish between what he had done for them and what they had done for him.

While Churchill, Attlee, Bevin and Eden watched the men file past them before joining their landing crafts, a member of his own union called out: 'Look after the missus and kids, Ernie.' Painfully aware of what awaited that man and thousands of others on the other side of the Channel, Bevin walked back to the car in tears.

No story illustrates better the affection people had for him or the confidence which they had in him. No story illustrates better the principles for which he stood or the soft heart which beat within his powerful frame.

As the parties prepared for a general election, speculation arose as to what Bevin might do. Several of his friends thought he might retire. Several political commentators thought he might be willing to join a nationally-based government under Churchill.

Neither were right. Bevin would have liked the Coalition to have continued until the defeat of Japan and then to have become Chancellor of the Exchequer if Labour won, Director General of the International Labour Organisation if defeated.

In the meantime in a forthright attack on the Conservatives he made his allegiance to the Labour Party crystal clear: 'A lot of the Tory propagandists seem to have forgotten that I am a member of the Labour Party,' he said in a speech in Leeds. 'I have been a member through all its vicissitudes.... As far as I am concerned I still abide by the Party decision – whatever it may be.' Then he went on to attack the Conservatives for their failure to oppose Hitler before the War and their failure to reduce the dole queue. (There was still more than one million unemployed in April 1940 when Bevin became Minister of Labour.) Finally he appealed for the public ownership of coal, electricity, gas and the Bank of England.

Privately it did not seem to affect his relations with Churchill. On 8 May, VE Day, the War Cabinet appeared on the balcony of the Ministry of Health before a huge crowd. When Churchill invited Bevin to come forward and share the applause with him, Bevin refused, saying: 'No, Winston, this is your day.'

He was, however, furious with Churchill for associating Socialism with the Gestapo in an election speech. Bevin thought Churchill must have been out of his mind. It appears that many of the electorate thought so too, since the result of the election was a landslide to Labour. They polled well over 3 million more votes than the Conservatives and won 393 seats in the greatest victory in their history.

On 27 May Attlee asked Bevin to be Foreign Secretary; not Chancellor of the Exchequer, as he had hoped. The offer came as a complete surprise. Later Attlee, who had also been encouraged by the King to appoint Bevin in the post, explained that he wanted 'a heavy tank' not 'a sniper' to deal with the Russians.

So that evening in company with the new Prime Minister Bevin was on a plane to Potsdam to meet Stalin and Truman. His seaside holiday in Devon with his wife Flo was cancelled, and the prospect of retirement, which he had so looked forward to more than five years ago, was no closer.

Chapter 12

Foreign Secretary

Bevin hoped to woo the Russians. He believed that 'Left would be able to speak to Left'. He also believed that he had earned a special right to their attention through his part in persuading the British Government not to provide the Poles direct help as they advanced across the Steppes into the rich farmlands of the Ukraine in 1920.

There was nothing naïve about this hope. He knew how difficult the Russians could be. Several frustrating experiences with their trade unions had proved this to him, and their territorial demands at Potsdam had confirmed it. But he hoped that when dealing with their leaders regularly he might eventually find a greater freedom to negotiate than he had with Soviet trade unionists. He once said to Stalin: 'We cannot help meeting in places and the thing for you and me to do is to keep the ball bearings so greased that there will be no friction when we do meet'; and it was in this spirit that he approached the problem of Anglo-Soviet relations.

What he hoped to do was to carry on the wartime alliance of Russia, the United States and Britain and so, through the offices of the 'Big Three',* secure an enduring settlement. But Britain's economic weakness, Russia's military strength and initially American susceptibility to Russian blandishments, conspired to defeat this design.

From the Americans Bevin received an unhelpful inheritance. Early in 1945 at Yalta, Roosevelt had declared that all American troops would have left Europe two years after victory. Then just before Bevin became Foreign Secretary,

* The 'Big Three' had become 'The Four' as a result of Potsdam when France had joined in, but France was economically far weaker than Britain.

Eisenhower and Truman agreed to surrender an area of some 400 miles long and 120 miles wide in Germany to Russian occupation against Churchill's advice and without gaining anything in return.

'Russia's interests so far as we can anticipate them,' said Harry L. Hopkins, Roosevelt's special envoy on his last mission to Moscow, 'do not afford an opportunity for a major difference with us in foreign affairs.' It was this American view of Russia's intentions, combined with Britain's economic and military weakness, which allowed the Russians to push forward their frontiers. Any aggressive or even defensive British noises both Russians and Americans alike considered the mutterings of erstwhile Imperialists.

Fortunately Bevin had learnt patience. He had developed as Francis Williams points out, 'a massive ability to bide his time, to keep his emotions under control and look beyond the immediate check to the unfolding future'. So despite rebuffs and constant hostility, Bevin, while in Moscow for a Foreign Ministers' meeting, tried to persuade Stalin to agree to extend the Anglo-Russian Treaty first drawn up during the War and to develop it into a 50-year alliance.

To this approach, so Bevin told his colleagues, Stalin replied: 'I should need to amend it.'

Bevin responded: 'Let me know what would suit you.'

But his initiative came to nothing. Attempts by two successive British ambassadors to find out what amendments the Russians sought never even led to full negotiations.

In his desire to build a diplomatic bridge between London and Moscow, Bevin did not, however, ignore the other avenues open to him to strengthen the country's position and prevent another war. With Europe, he sought military alliance and gradual economic development. Through the United Nations he sought an international resolve for world peace. From the United States he hoped to stimulate a new lead.

Early in 1946 the French Prime Minister, Monsieur Felix Gouin, proposed the signing of an Anglo-French treaty as a first step towards European unity. Although only a symbol of friendship and military support, Bevin responded enthusiastically and in March the two countries signed a 50-year pact at Dunkirk – a place chosen to signify a joint determination to survive.

The Brussels Treaty followed in 1948. This was a far more elaborate military agreement involving the Low Countries as well as France and Britain. Headquarters were set up in Fontainebleau. The Chiefs of Staff Committee was put under the leadership of Field Marshal Montgomery. Later it was to become the nucleus for NATO.

But the Russians' hostility to Britain and advances beyond their traditional frontiers, still led Bevin to the reluctant but firm conclusion that the whole of Europe and the Middle East would remain vulnerable to Soviet threat until protected by the United States. To bring the United States back to Europe and to coax her into a major international peacekeeping role became his top priority.

This was a far from easy task. Few Americans believed that the Russians had any 'crazy ideas of conquest' They still suspected Britain of harbouring thoughts of imperialism. On the one hand, they thought she exaggerated her economic difficulties; on the other, they feared her as a trading rival. Nor could they see any advantage to themselves in contributing to European re-construction.

As news of the extent of Russia's influence over her neighbours reached the United States and American opinion began to appreciate the degree of her ambition, Bevin looked for a moment in which to turn sympathy into solid support. That opportunity first came in 1947 when Russia increased pressure on Turkey to cede her border states to the Soviet Union and lease her naval bases on the Bosphorus. At the same time guerilla warfare flared up again in Greece.

On the afternoon of 21 February 1947 the British Embassy in Washington, on Bevin's instructions, abruptly informed George C. Marshall, US Secretary of State, that in view of her economic difficulties she could no longer provide adequate assistance to preserve the status quo in these two countries. If they were to be supported, Britain could not manage alone. America would have to play a part.

Judged by what happened next, Bevin's carefully timed intervention must rate as one of the most decisive acts in the history of diplomacy: the State Department decided that Great Britain had 'handed the job of world leadership with all its burdens and all its glories to the United States'. That was precisely what Bevin was trying to do. But the result exceeded his expectations. Not only did President Truman persuade Congress to vote $400 million worth of aid for these two countries, but also to endorse an international policy which ended isolationism. The policy which became known as the 'Truman Doctrine' undertook to support 'free peoples who are resisting attempted subjugation by armed minorities or outside pressure'.

'If we falter we may endanger the peace of the world,' Truman continued, 'and we shall surely endanger the welfare of our own nation.' From this moment onwards, Bevin knew that there would be no vacuum, where Britain had to withdraw.

This American initiative, however, was only the first of two in which Bevin played a significant part in the space of three months. The second occurred on 7 June.

On that morning Bevin had, as usual, woken early; certainly not later than 5 o'clock. Surrounded by his dispatch boxes which littered his bed, he had worked for a couple of hours, before pausing to listen to the news on the wireless. After the main news of the day, there was a brief reference to a speech made by George C. Marshall, the US Secretary of State, at Harvard University, which suggested that America would be prepared to help Europe financially, if the European countries got together and put forward a programme.

The news bulletin did not give many details. So in his bedroom slippers, Bevin went to seek confirmation from the morning papers. On the front page of the *Daily Herald*, his own paper, he was pleased to see that the *Herald*'s Washington Correspondent reported the speech at some length.

As he read it, one sentence stood out in bold relief: 'The initiative must come from Europe.... When European countries have agreed on their requirements and on the part they themselves will play, then – and only then – can the United States take supporting action.'

Cogitating on what he had heard and what he had read, the offer seemed to Bevin 'like a lifeline to sinking men'. Then he began to think about the response the Foreign Office might make.

The first man to knock on Bevin's door at the Foreign Office that morning was Sir William (later Lord) Strang, his Permanent Under Secretary. Strang had also read the speech and according to Dean Acheson in his book *Sketches from Life*, had come to suggest that Bevin instruct the Washington Embassy to inquire of the State Department what General Marshall meant by his speech.

'Bill,' Bevin said, 'if you ask questions, you'll get answers you don't want. Our problem is what we do, not what he meant.'

From that exchange came the decision to instruct the British Ambassador to express Britain's deep appreciation of the offer made by the US Government and inform the State Department that the Foreign Office was in the process of consulting with the French Foreign Minister to see how best the offer could be implemented.

Then another thought struck Bevin. Close inspection of the text of the speech revealed that Marshall had not specifically excluded the Russians. Russia was part of Europe. If Russia could be persuaded to join in, perhaps after all the 'Iron Curtain' might be gently drawn back and, through trade, a better understanding emerge.

So Bevin got in touch with Molotov who agreed to meet the British and French Foreign Ministers in Paris. 'Perhaps they will play after all,' he kept repeating in the Foreign

Office. Full of hope, in the House of Commons he described Marshall's speech as 'one of the greatest speeches in world history'.

On 18 June Molotov, Bidault and Bevin met in Paris. It was not a constructive meeting. Molotov* wanted to know how much the Americans were prepared to offer. He objected to aid being given to ex-enemy countries until the needs of other European countries had been satisfied. He could not believe that the offer was only conditional upon joint European co-operation. In sum, the Russians suspected a trick and ended up, after withdrawing, describing the offer as a threat. In the process, they made themselves particularly unpopular with the Czechoslovaks who had wished to take advantage of Marshall's offer and who were now, under Soviet pressure, forced to withdraw.

With Russia out of it, 14 other nations met in Paris on 12 July. There they formed the Committee of European Economic Co-operation and by the end of September had succeeded in presenting Marshall with a four-year plan for European reconstruction.

For Western Europe it proved the lifeline Bevin hoped it might be. Over a period of four years the United States poured $17,000 billion into Europe. Even by 1950 pre-war production levels had increased by 25%. As Sked and Cook say in their book *Post-War Britain*, America had achieved a 'brilliant diplomatic success and engineered a domestic economic boom'.

For Bevin it was a partial triumph. On the one hand, Marshall graciously acknowledged later that he had not fully appreciated what he had let the United States in for. In this respect his prompt reaction and powerful words played a significant part in extending American generosity. On the other hand, Russian rejection of the American offer and par-

* Of Molotov, Bevin once said: 'If you treated him badly he made the most of his grievance and if you treated him well he only put up his price and abused you next day.'

ticularly her insistence upon Czechoslovakian withdrawal, exacerbated the division between Russia and Western Europe.

Two events in 1948 highlighted the insecurity of Europe. In February the Czechoslovak Communist Party overthrew by coup d'état the democratically elected Government of Eduard Benes. In March the Russians imposed restrictions on rail traffic coming into Berlin and three months later imposed a complete blockade.

The 'Rape of Czechoslovakia', as it came to be called, shocked the world. In May 1946 the Communists had won 114 of the 300 seats in the Duma. Since then popular sentiment had hardened against the Communists partly because the Government reversed, under Soviet pressure, an earlier decision to accept aid under the Marshall Plan, partly because the Minister of the Interior was filling all senior police posts with Communists.

Just before new elections, due in May, the Communists seized power and on the very day that a unanimous vote of confidence was given to them, Jan Masaryk, the Foreign Minister, was found dead under his window in the Czernin Palace. His suicide or murder caused a wave of horror throughout the 'free world'.

Politically the Berlin blockade had an even greater impact. It brought the world to the brink of a third world war. From that city General Clay, the American commander, reported to Washington: 'A new tenseness in every Soviet individual with whom we have official relations. . . . gives me a feeling that war may come with dramatic suddenness.'

The Russians justified the blockade on the grounds that the allies had no right to introduce a new currency in their zones of occupation under present arrangements. This was a means to get the West to give up their part of Berlin or alternatively to give them bargaining power to wrest another slice of Austria for the Communist bloc. In fact they were gambling on what seemed a reasonable assumption that the West had no means of breaking the Blockade of this tiny outpost of Western democracy surrounded by Soviet occupied territory.

Faced with this challenge neither Britain nor America hesitated. As Mark Arnold Foster says in his book *The World at War*: 'In 1948 no one supposed that it would be possible to supply 2¼ million city dwellers with food, fuel and raw materials for their industries by air. But two Western statesmen in particular thought it could be done: President Truman and the British Foreign Secretary, Ernest Bevin.'

The struggle lasted 324 days. By joint Anglo-American effort, over 200,000 flights brought in more than 1½ million tons of supplies. In the Commons Bevin said: 'It showed conclusively that the people of Berlin did not want to fall into dependence upon Soviet Russia, since they knew that this was the first step of subjection.'

These events made a tremendous impact on Europe and America. No longer could the Russians explain them away as a search for security. They were patently aggressive, premeditated attempts to extend their hegemony. Throughout the Western world there was a call for 'a new adjustment of power' and the United States indicated her willingness to play an active part in the defence of the West.

Ten months later the North Atlantic Treaty, the fruit of all these initiatives, had been drawn up. On 4 April 1949 Bevin, on behalf of the United Kingdom, signed the Treaty with 11 other countries. It was, so he told Francis Williams, 'one of the greatest moments of all my life'. He called it: 'The biggest step of collective security in the history of the world.'

In his address Bevin said: 'This pact is a concrete proof of the determination of a group of like-minded nations never to fight one another. These nations are, in addition, linked with many other people who equally will never indulge in aggression. All these peoples are united in a common line of thought and desire.

'Today is not only the day of the signature of this pact; it is also a day of solemn thought – and, may I say, of consecration for peace and resistance to aggression.'

These were not just pious words. The pact was, and is still today, a defensive treaty. It is quite unlike the 'Truman Doctrine' which promised help to people struggling to win freedom. Constitutionally, therefore, its signatories under its name can theoretically provide no military help outside its frontiers.

To Bevin the North Atlantic Treaty was the climax of his working life. In its construction he believed he had played a major part in setting up an organisation that would contribute to peace; that would allow 'the common people ... unable to follow their peaceful pursuits ... to sleep safely in their beds'.

What is so amazing about Bevin's successes with the Americans is that he achieved them against a background of one of the most frustrating and complicated international situations that the two countries ever had to deal with: Palestine. At any time during the first two years after the War, any diplomatic move on the part of Britain, however sound, could have been upset by the failure of the two countries to find a solution to this intractable problem.

Palestine had become a British responsibility in 1918 when it was put under British administration by a League of Nations mandate. It was not a straightforward administrative job of government, however. Through the Balfour Declaration, the British had undertaken to establish a national home for the Jewish people on the understanding that the civil and religious rights of the non-Jewish communities were preserved.

After the Second World War, Palestine held a magnetic pull for hundreds of thousands of Jews who had survived the Nazi holocaust, and they expected immediate and unconditional right of entry to the land of their fathers. Without full regard to the needs and rights of the Palestinians they felt that the least that the International Community could do for them was to give them back their native land.

It was Bevin's unenviable task to administer the Mandate;

to rule on such agonising questions as the level of Jewish immigration and arbitrate on the terms on which the new Israel might become an independent state.

Bevin tried to treat the issue in many respects as the TUC treats an inter-union dispute, taking no sides. In November 1945, with President Truman's help, he set up an Anglo-American committee of inquiry. His aim was to get agreement from both sides, and refuse to make any changes until that agreement was forthcoming.

But its recommendations, although eventually unanimous, pleased nobody; neither Jew, nor Arab, nor – what is more – American. It pleased nobody because it did not come out clearly for either a Jewish state or an Arab state. Instead it recommended the entry of an additional 100,000 Jews, but what was of acute embarrassment to the British Government, it did not rule that this entry should be conditional upon Jewish disarmament. Had the Committee done so, it would not have been a unanimous report.

Bevin then made what many people consider to be his greatest blunder. He ruled that liquidation of private armies had to come before the entry of the 100,000. This caused total deadlock and a considerable escalation of terrorism. Bevin's case was not helped by President Truman who welcomed the report without taking any account whatever of the views of the British Foreign Secretary.

Once Bevin had made up his mind that he was right he always stuck firm, as trade union, employer and government alike could testify; and on this issue he stuck firm. The result was a rapid deterioration in relations between the Jews and the British and a carefully planned terrorist campaign culminating in the blowing-up of the King David Hotel in Jerusalem with tragic loss of life.

Regardless of whether Bevin was right or wrong this decision severely damaged the relationship between the United States and Britain. Liberally both sides traded insults. The Americans accused the British of wanting to hold on to Palestine because of her oil interests. They also accused

Britain of being pro-Arab. The British suggested that the Americans only wanted a Jewish homeland to keep the Jews out of New York, and to help win elections.

Mercifully on 2 April 1947 Bevin decided to refer the problem to the United Nations. On 14 May 1948 the British ignominiously withdrew and the new State of Israel was born; on terms which Bevin thought were both unfair and had little chance of long-term success.

In this tragic story, however, one thing needs stressing. Bevin was not anti-Jewish. From 1920 until the War, the Bevins had lived in Golders Green and many of their friends were Jews. Moreover while trying to solve the problems in Palestine he consulted representatives of British Jewry and thought that with them he could have found the basis of a settlement which included recognition of the needs of the Palestinians. Moreover, in supporting the Labour candidate in a Whitechapel bye-election in 1930 he had issued a statement passing on the explicit assurance of the Labour Government that they had no intention of stopping immigration or of setting limits to the expansion of the Jewish National Home within the terms of the Mandate.

Eventually the Council of Europe was set up in 1949. But in spite of the fact that Bevin had advocated a united states of Europe as far back as 1926 in Milwaukee, years before Churchill's first utterance on the subject, he was not enamoured of the prospect. 'If you open that Pandora's Box you never know what Trojan horses will jump out,' he said of it.

There were two reasons for this. First Bevin had suffered a number of bad experiences at the hands of loose federations where the freedoms of individual constituents were incompatible with the aims of the organisation. In 1920 the Triple Alliance had sunk without trace, and in 1926 the General Strike had failed for this very reason.

'I am not a very strong believer in Constitutions. I like the thing that grows, the thing that evolves,' Bevin was to say in an argument over the respective roles of the Council of

Ministers and the Assembly, according to Sir Roderick Barclay, his Private Secretary.

The second reason was equally practical. According to Lord Strang, his Permanent Under-Secretary during Bevin's last year as Foreign Secretary, in his book *Home and Abroad*: 'The Consultative Assembly, beloved of Parliamentarians, seemed to him to be merely another forum where elected representatives could go and make more speeches; and the Committee of Ministers, as he saw it, lacked the prime purpose for which international bodies should be set up, namely, a precise and concrete job of work to do.'

In other words if European unity developed like the Transport and General Workers' Union, slowly and deliberately evolving into a powerful giant, then he was for it. If all that it was likely to become was a huge bureaucratic machine without effective power or clear purpose he was against it.

In contrast to the part he played in creating the Council of Europe, Bevin threw his full weight behind the United Nations. He believed that it could become a far more effective body than the League of Nations in which the Labour Movement had placed such faith between the Wars. To this end, Bevin was prepared to take infinite trouble to ensure that the United Kingdom supported it and helped it develop into the premier forum for world peace.

What he looked to the United Nations to do was to launch a world-wide attack on poverty by increasing the flow of primary products to under-developed countries, and by putting essential raw materials under international control. Since the 1930s he had regularly repeated his deeply-held conviction that raw materials must be supervised to prevent war and his unfailing attendance of all key meetings at the United Nations during his six years as Foreign Secretary indicates what store he set by this new organisation.

His thinking ran like this: as the clue to world peace lay in political and social equality, no country had a greater responsibility for realising this aim than the United Kingdom because of her past empire. However, having sacrificed her export trade and her overseas investments during the War, she was in no position to provide the economic assistance many of her dominions and colonies desperately needed. If, by some means, the United Nations could become an effective policeman where there was conflict and an effective support where there was need, then the problems facing the United Kingdom would assume a different shape.

But the Russians believed that the wrecking of Britain's reputation at the UN was essential to smooth their advance in Europe and the Middle East. So wherever Britain was involved – in Greece, Iran and Palestine, for example – Russia hurled insults about her imperial ambition from the rostrum of the Security Council. Yet despite all this, ignoring American pressure, Bevin still insisted on Britain recognising Communist China.

Bevin bore these attacks with fortitude. He never gave up hope of 'rapprochement', in spite of the number of Russian vetoes which so weakened the effectiveness of the UN. Nor did he ever lose his optimism. 'If peace breaks out anywhere, I'll give you a ring', he used to say cheerily as he left the Foreign Office for another interminable negotiating session with the Russians.

In parallel with Bevin's work at the UN was his work at the International Labour Organisation (ILO) in Geneva which became a special UN agency in 1946. Bevin considered the ILO an essential component in his search for peace. While General-Secretary of the TGWU he made several visits to Geneva and in 1929, for example, was instrumental in drawing up an international code for the prevention of accidents in the loading and unloading of ships.

During the War Bevin chaired the emergency committee meeting of the ILO in London in 1942 at which he declared: 'This is a people's war: it must lead to a people's peace.'

121

This caught the imagination of the Press and the *Manchester Guardian* wrote that 'more directly than any other British minister he (Bevin) faced the fact that the peace will be a revolutionary peace.'

Throughout the War Bevin was to keep up his support of the ILO. According to Bullock, Bevin's championing of the ILO had a significant consequence: 'When the time came to set up the new world organisation in the United Nations, he was able to put the full weight of the British Government's support behind the ILO's claim to be given a proper place among the other specialised agencies, and the success of the ILO in surviving the war and maintaining its identity owed more to Bevin's efforts on its behalf than to those of any other single person, in Britain or in any other country.'

After the War the ILO set up a number of industrial committees for coal-mining, building, oil, chemicals etc. In G. A. Johnston's history of the ILO he says: 'It is due to the far-sighted statesmanship and deep understanding of the potentialities of the ILO shown by Ernest Bevin ... that the Industrial Committees came into being.' In the 1950s and 1960s these tri-partite committees involving government, employers and trade unions increased both in number and importance adding such vital subjects as civil aviation and hotels, amply vindicating the support he had given the ILO since 1928, when he first represented the dockers at one of their meetings.

Bevin's final achievement as Foreign Secretary was the first conference ever held of Commonwealth Foreign Ministers in the Sinhalese capital of Colombo. Bevin had always been a strong believer in the potential value of the Commonwealth, and the purpose of the meeting was not only to nurture the relationship which already existed but also to develop a positive strategy which would give this loose association of friendly nations a common purpose.

From this meeting emerged the Colombo Plan – an Asian equivalent of the Marshall Plan – with the aim of providing moncy, advice and technical training to the less-developed members of the Commonwealth. By 1951 this had developed into a major scheme involving the United States who, in the same generous way as they had done for Europe, contributed more than half the funds.

The meeting in Colombo had taken place in 1950. Bevin was to remain Foreign Secretary for another year, but his health was deteriorating due to his heart condition. Walking tended to bring on a heart attack and climbing stairs was almost impossible. Unless Alec McCall, his Scottish doctor, was near at hand, his health became a real anxiety to his officials.

But Bevin was not going to give up. He was quite prepared to go into hospital every weekend in order to conserve and build up his strength for the week. This was not just the determination of a man unwilling to retire. Nobody has ever suggested that his illness clouded his judgement and he believed – and so did many others – that he was the best man to steer the nation through the Korean War and the problems, for example, in the Canal Zone.

So when Attlee told him on his 70th birthday that he wished to move Bevin from the Foreign Office and make him Lord Privy Seal, Bevin was deeply upset. 'I am neither a Lord, nor a privy, nor a seal,' he said. Later, under stress of deep emotion, he said to Lord Strang: 'I was born into a poor little home and went to a poor little school, and look what I have done in the world. There must be some purpose in it. And now they want to throw me on the scrap-heap.'

In fact he was far from being a broken man. When he got to grips with the work of the Lord Privy Seal, his optimism quickly returned. Amongst other things he was responsible for Welsh affairs. This involved renewing acquaintance with old friends such as Huw T. Edwards, the TGWU official in North Wales for whom he promised to do 'something really creative for Wales'.

On 14 April 1951 he was due to go with his wife, daughter and son-in-law to watch the home international at Wembley between England and Scotland. He was not well enough to go. But he insisted on his family going and told his daughter Que to remember who scored the goals. While they were out, he worked on his papers. His last act was to ask a friend to close his dispatch boxes for him. Then he died.

Conclusion

No Englishman in history has risen from such humble origins to such high office, or contributed so much to the world from so deprived a background as Ernest Bevin.

Of all Labour leaders, not even Keir Hardie can boast quite such an inauspicious beginning as Bevin. He was born illegitimate, the seventh child of a widow. He knew no father. At the age of eight he was orphaned.

His education was minimal and he never acquired a skill. Whenever he dictated to a secretary, she had to 'put it into English'. Whenever he spoke in the House of Commons '*ex tempor*', as he described an off-the-cuff speech, a civil servant had to tidy up *Hansard* without changing the sense in order to make his sentences grammatical.

Apart from his membership of the Bristol Socialist Society, his early life hardly suggests what was to follow. He moved from farm to refreshment rooms, from the trams to a laundry without any obvious reason other than a desire for a change. On more than one occasion he was unemployed. Even at the age of 30 he was still driving a cart delivering mineral water.

That this immensely tough and ill-educated farm labourer from the borders of Exmoor should have become the greatest trade unionist, the greatest Minister of Labour and arguably the greatest Foreign Secretary this century is amazing. His rise must rank as one of the greatest achievements in the history of human endeavour.

What made this manual worker into the creator of the most powerful union in the country and then into a legendary Minister of the Crown? I believe there were three basic influences: a Christian conviction, a Socialist conversion and the experience of success which bred more success.

The Christian conviction is the most difficult to write

about. In the possession of Bevin's daughter Que there are two of his bibles. In one there is the inscription: 'Ernest Bevin entered into the fullness of Christ', signed by a Minister with 200 verses underlined by the Minister, and dated 10 February 1904.

On its own that would be little evidence of a deep faith amounting to a life-long influence. But in the other bible, written in Bevin's unmistakably halting hand, there is the following:

'I This evening Sept 18th 1907 I have resolved By the Grace of God to serve him where ever he may call me. may God keep me an gaurd me till he shall call me home'
singed Ernest Bevin Sept 18th 1907.

This was three and a half years later than the first inscription and has all the marks of a genuine reflection of what he believed. His daughter says: 'My Father never spoke about his faith, but I know it was important to him. He had this bible next to his bed, and he used to read it every night. Occasionally at home he used to quote quite long passages from it.' Moreover as a family they were regular church-goers, although in the later years not members of any particular congregation.*

The origins of his Socialism were simpler. He first drove a cart round the Bristol area in 1901. What he saw on his rounds shocked him and made him angry: poverty cheek by jowl with great riches. For several years he accepted it, presumably believing that the Church would stir the consciences of the rich while at the same time lifting the spirits of the poor.

---

* Bevin once told Dean Acheson, American Secretary of State, that he was a 'bush' Baptist. Acheson said that he did not understand the word. Bevin told Acheson to ask President Truman whom Bevin knew to be a Baptist. Truman explained to Acheson that a 'bush' Baptist was a Baptist from the hills, so called as a protest against the decadence of the cities. It was rather an appropriate description in view of Bevin's background.

Then one day, frustrated by the lack of progress in the lot of the poor, he told his Baptist Minister that he could not go on preaching God to people who had empty stomachs and had joined the Bristol Socialist Society to do something about it. It was probably about this time that he threw a huge pat of butter at his employer after being caught giving a poor family more butter than they had paid for.

At the outset and for many years Bevin's Socialism was very aggressive. It burnt deep into his soul, as the following statement of his from a meeting of employers and trade unions under the chairmanship of the Lord Mayor of Bristol in January 1917 shows:

'I had to work at ten years of age while my employer's son went to the university until he was twenty. You have set out for me a different set of conditions. I was taught to bow to the squire and touch my hat to the parson; my employer's son was not. All these things have produced within me an intense hatred, a hatred which has caused me to organise for my fellows and direct my mind to a policy to give my class a power to control their own destiny and labour.'

As the years went by the language in which he couched his Socialism became more moderate, but his Socialist conviction remained in much the same way as his Christian conviction did. On several occasions during the War he tried to persuade Churchill to repeal the 1927 Trade Disputes Act, particularly those sections preventing the Civil Service Unions affiliating to the TUC. Besides, the raising of minimum wage levels and the introduction of Joint Industrial Councils with management and trade unions participating on equal terms, for which he was responsible during the War, can hardly be construed as the first fruits of the High Tory mind. Yet the Left Wing of the Labour Party suspected he had abandoned his Socialism and was firmly in the pocket of Churchill.

As Foreign Secretary too one of his overriding motivations was to help the common people of the world; to support 'peasants not pashas' as one celebrated Foreign Office memorandum put it. So Rab Butler's quip about him: 'Hasn't

Anthony Eden grown fat?' was only a fair description, in so far as there was a deliberate post-war attempt not to make foreign policy a party issue.

So these two influences – Christianity in the background, Socialism at the forefront – came together and spurred the young Bevin into action. After his first success as the leader of the Bristol 'Right-to-Work' campaign which resulted in the City Council spending more money on public works he grew more confident with every success until invited by Churchill into the War Cabinet as Minister of Labour and National Service in 1940.

However the most telling of his achievements was the creation of the Transport and General Workers Union. Launched on the first day of 1922 this was the foundation stone on which he built the rest of his career. Transport House, its headquarters, became a kind of spiritual home to him. If he was ever back late from lunch during his ten and a half years in government, his officials knew they could always find him there.

The TGWU was important to Bevin not just because he founded it, nor just because it provided him with massive support, but primarily because of what he had been and what it represented. He had been an unskilled man and it was an unskilled union representing those who had nowhere else to go for representation.* Bevin belonged to and never wished to dissociate himself from the Union. 'The first British statesman to have been born a working man and remained one,' was the *Observer*'s tribute at the end of the War.

This did not mean that he felt uncomfortable in the company of those with different backgrounds. Indeed he felt perfectly comfortable and naturally treated them as equals. That is what he wanted for himself and that is what he wanted for all the members of his Union. 'He thought he was

* 'In one town I organize the midwives, in another the grave diggers and everything between is the Transport Workers,' Bevin once told an employer who had asked him why on earth he was doing recruiting union members in his factory.

128

as good as anyone else in the country and he saw no reason why everybody should not have the same high opinion of himself,' wrote Attlee in 1960.

Royalty he treated in the same way. They seemed to like his lack of deference. Queen Mary was a great admirer. She gave Bevin a key to the garden of Marlborough House, while he was in the Foreign Secretary's residence in Carlton Gardens. For his seventieth birthday she also gave him an elaborate Victorian lace fan to help him keep cool, when suffering from an attack of angina.

His relations with King George VI were also intimate. They met frequently and after the Labour victory in 1945 King George wrote to his brother the Duke of Gloucester: 'My new Government is not too easy and the people are rather difficult to talk to. Bevin is very good and tells me everything that is going on.' On a number of occasions when Sir Roderick Barclay saw them together: 'Ernie would put a large hand on the King's back and lead him to a corner where he would tell him some story which usually evoked roars of laughter.'

There is also a legend that when Bevin went to kiss hands on his appointment as Minister of Labour in 1940, Bevin's reply to a question from King George about how he managed to acquire such knowledge of public affairs, was: 'Sir, it was gathered in the hedgerows of experience.'

Bevin's other connection with royalty was a full length portrait of King George III which hung behind his desk in the Foreign Office. Unlike George Brown who had it taken down, Bevin thought it was a huge joke to have the most imperialist of English monarchs for his visitors to gaze at.

' 'e's my hero,' he would say to American visitors. 'Let's drink to 'im. If 'e hadn't been so stoopid, you wouldn't have been strong enough to come to our rescue in the War.'

But he himself would not accept honours (although he was quite prepared to put forward other people's names). Ramsay MacDonald offered Bevin a peerage during his second government. Bevin turned it down. At the end of the Second World

War Churchill recommended him for a Companion of Honour. The following day Bevin replied: 'I have given the matter careful consideration and whilst ... I thank you for your suggestion, I prefer not to accept. The job I have undertaken, like thousands of others, ... has been in the interests of the Nation and I do not desire special Honours.'

Bevin extended his desire to be treated on equal terms into every walk of life both private and professional. So when Vyshinsky turned up at a meeting of Foreign Ministers to replace Molotov and admitted to Bevin at one stage in the proceedings that he was unable to negotiate as: 'I have my instructions', Bevin would not even talk to him. According to Harold Nicolson, Bevin said: 'Well, I have no instructions other than those which I give to myself. Clearly, therefore we are not discussing on the same level, and I had better turn you over to my deputy.' 'Vyshinsky blinked at that,' Nicolson records, 'but he could go no further. Therefore the meeting broke pending Molotov's return.'

In much the same way Bevin earned a remarkable reputation for keeping his word however inconvenient it might prove at the time. 'Once his word was given,' wrote Oliver Lyttelton, Minister of Production in the War Cabinet, 'nothing would shake it: it had the cachet of a guarantee by the Bank of England.'

This aspect of his character again needs to be understood in a union context. An undertaking from Bevin was not easy to come by. He did not offer a promise until the matter concerned had been thoroughly discussed, and the implications of making a commitment considered. Then and only then would he give his word, but once given he personally considered it binding. Throughout the world he became famous for his dependability in this respect.

To Bevin this was not just a matter of morality, but also of common sense. A union could have no confidence in its strength, unless a collective decision, once reached, was invariably honoured. It was a principle to which Bevin religiously adhered and he expected every member of the Union to do the same. Any deviation from this principle he described as treachery and he ruthlessly dealt with offenders.

Outside the Union Bevin applied the same rules both to himself and everybody else. In 1935 Bevin pitilessly attacked Lansbury for arguing publicly against a decision to which he was party. During the Second World War for a long period, Bevin would not speak to those members of the Labour Party who would not support the Coalition Government to which they had committed themselves. At no point during his life was he willing to set this principle aside for the sake of convenience.

However this stringent application of loyalty to a collective decision pre-supposed free and open discussion in the first place. This freedom was just as precious to Bevin. As Bullock says in his life of Bevin:

'Bevin's life was lived in an atmosphere of discussion and uninhibited argument. His power derived from his ability to carry his Executive, the Biennial Delegate Conference and ultimately the rank-and-file members of the Union with him, a fact which he never for one moment forgot.'

In fact Bevin revelled in free discussion and his encouragement of it both at the Ministry of Labour and within the Foreign Office is one of the reasons why his colleagues found him so exciting to work with. 'Ha,' said Bevin to one colleague who returned for further discussion on a subject, 'the ink is hardly dry on the words of my mouth, and here you are again.' So in this respect too he was applying principles which were fundamental to the Union in a wider context.

In fact Bevin loved to talk and he loved to laugh. He was excellent company – when he did not have something like the Berlin blockade on his mind – and a first class story-teller. Few of his stories survive, however, and anyhow lose a great deal without Bevin himself to tell them. But one retrieved by Peter Ustinov and recounted in his autobiography 'Dear Me' is characteristic:

'There was three men in a boat, see, a Communist, a Fascist and a good Union man. All of a sudden the boat sinks and the three men are thrown in the water. There's people on the river bank. The Fascist salutes at them, but finds it impossible to swim with one arm, and 'e drowns. The Communist begins shouting slogans at them, exhausts 'imself, and 'e drowns. This leaves only the Union man, swimmin' towards the bank in strong easy strokes. He's almost within 'is depth, when the factory siren goes and 'e drowns.'

About Bevin himself, there are countless stories which still circulate in the Foreign Office. There is the one about his first introduction to caviar which evoked the comment: 'This jam tastes fishy.' There's another about the complete lack of comprehension on a waiter's face when Bevin asked him for a 'bottle of newts' which the waiter subsequently discovered after a little interpretation meant 'Nuits St Georges'. But maybe Bevin was just playing up to his audience on these occasions, in the same way as he deliberately dropped his aitches for particularly posh audiences.

There was a rugged charm about him which won the hearts of all who came into contact with him. According to Lord Strang, Bevin discovered at a lunch at the Iraqi Embassy in London on St David's Day, 1950 that Lady Strang was of Welsh ancestry. So gathering a bunch of daffodils from the centre of the table he rose to his feet, presented them to her with a graceful little speech of congratulation and then proposed a toast to Wales.

Most of his social confidence must be attributed to the happiness of his home. Here Bevin was able to relax when he could get away from the demands of work. His tastes were simple and his requirements few. He and his wife Flo shared an interest in religion – they had first met at chapel – and music hall. Flo had one persistent foible. She liked to change the layout of the rooms often, and expected her husband to move the furniture for her.

Between the Wars the Bevins lived in Golders Green at 30 The Vale. This was the only time in his life when his hours were remotely normal and the time when his daughter Que got to know him best. She remembers him telling her stories, playing whist and monopoly and listening to Caruso, Marie Lloyd or Clara Butt on the gramophone.

If he had a weekend free he would go to the Turkish baths in Jermyn Street immediately after leaving work on Saturday afternoon. Then in the evening he would take Flo and Q to the local music hall and afterwards out to a meal. On Sunday they would go for a drive. Bevin loved driving and his favourite car was a big yellow Talbot Darracq. Together they would drive out into the country until they had found a good spot for a walk. Then, leaving Flo with a newspaper, Bevin and Que would roam the fields looking for animals and inspecting the crops.

He was much more interested in football than cricket, having played football on the dockside in Bristol. If they happened to be at home on Saturday, he would get out his crystal wireless set and tune in to the match on a pair of headphones. His team was Chelsea and nobody dared interrupt if Chelsea were playing.

His other great love was horses. Because he had worked with them as a carter for the best part of a decade, he knew a great deal about them. As a lad he had often followed hounds, but never ridden. In London he never missed the Whitsun Horse Show in Regent's Park and had as much confidence in picking a winning 'Shire' as in knowing the moment to launch a new initiative on behalf of his members. Later he was to take a particular interest in a home for retired horses, run by a Lady Warwick.

For holidays he liked to go to the sea. He could not swim, but he would always get into the water. The Bevins had no special resort to which they regularly returned. But the direction was always West – to Swanage, Torquay or West Wales. Occasionally they went on a cruise with the Workers Travel Association of which at one time Bevin was president.

His biographers say that he read little and could barely write. This is not true. He read a great deal more than he is given credit for. Not only was he occasionally seen with a book on his cart in Bristol, but according to his daughter was also well versed in Trollope and Dickens. Moreover he could not possibly have quoted from 'Old Salisbury' or 'Old Palmerston' in the way that he did, had he not been a reader. His writing, on the other hand, was a different story. He held his pen, which the Foreign Office nick-named the 'Caber' because of its size, between his second and third fingers and found writing quite uncomfortable. This was not because he could not write but because he had injured his index finger early in his life and had almost totally destroyed the nerves in it.

His untutored mind had two quite remarkable characteristics. It would soak up information and reproduce it to an accuracy which would astonish the most brilliant academic. The Foreign Office were constantly surprised at how reliable he was when stating facts. His other characteristic was an ability to put forward ideas. 'I like to create,' he once said; and on another occasion, 'I am a bit of a dreamer'. This made him exciting to work with and many of his colleagues say that their time working with him was the most stimulating of their lives. 'He swarmed with ideas,' one colleague said of him. This openness also had the effect of inspiring devotion.

Some found him egotistical, particularly Walter Citrine, General-Secretary of the TUC, who once said so in writing. This is partly true in that he referred to the *Daily Herald* as 'my paper', his union members as 'my people' and foreign policy as 'my policy'. On the other hand he occasionally pushed his staff to the forefront as was the case with George Tomlinson, his Labour parliamentary secretary, whom he made chairman of the committee set up to report on the rehabilitation of the disabled, because of the work Tomlinson had done on the preparation of the report.

His worst aspect was his inability to tolerate peers in the union world. He never ceased to be cold towards Walter Citrine throughout his career in spite of the fact that Citrine* invariably saw eye to eye with him on matters of policy. Had

---

* Citrine once said that he had never met Bevin's equal nor his superior in negotiation.

they worked as a team the trade unions might have made even greater strides before the War.

On the other hand, with Attlee Bevin forged one of the most successful partnerships in modern British politics. Attlee thrived on the loyal support which Bevin invariably gave him, Bevin thrived on the confidence which Attlee reposed in him. Consequently few Foreign Secretaries have ever enjoyed such freedom and respect as Bevin.

The soundness of their relationship and the closeness of their friendship put Bevin in a unique position. Other Foreign Secretaries and heads of state knew that, if Bevin made a pronouncement, behind it there lay unparalleled support, from the Trade Union Movement, the Labour Party and, above all, the Prime Minister.

At home their partnership, although less evident, was just as potent. As William Golant has pointed out in a recent article in *The Times* their compatability 'generated a definite impression of strength and moral resolve, competence and optimism.' The internecine warfare which broke out within the Labour Party after Bevin's death in 1951 and which had not occurred before, proved just how good this relationship had been for the Labour Government.

Bevin's relations with Dean Acheson, American Secretary of State, whom Bevin always called 'me lad', were as good and as decisive in foreign affairs. Together they worked on the Marshall Plan, the Berlin Airlift, the formation of NATO and the Colombo Plan in remarkable harmony.

When Bevin died Acheson captured more accurately than any other world statesman, the qualities which made Bevin one of the greatest figures of the twentieth century: 'His indomitable courage, his simplicity and directness, his love of his country and his understanding of the grandeur of its contribution to the cause of human liberty, his humanity and knowledge of the struggles and aspirations of his fellow men, his own warm affectionate good humour made him both loved and trusted. All of us to whom freedom and liberty are the foundation of our lives will stand in gratitude and joy that in these times such a man has lived.'

So, pulling all the manifold facets of Bevin's life together, what does it amount to? He built a union. He helped rescue a party. He mobilised a nation; then he made it secure. He set out to serve the common man, he ended up serving mankind. He stands a massive inspiration to all of us, particularly those without any advantage to their name.

Datelist

	Career	Events
1881	Born 7 March	
1889	Orphaned	Great London Dock Strike
1892	Farm Labourer	
1894	Moved to Bristol	
1908	Carter. Joins Bristol 'Right to Work' Committee	
1911	Full-time official of Docker's Union	Liverpool Dock Strike
1913	Assistant National Organiser. Moves to London	
1914	National Organiser	First World War
1915	Visits USA	
1917		Russian Revolution
1920		Shaw Inquiry. Council of Action
1921		'Black Friday'
1922	First General Secretary of TGWU	Transport & General Workers Union founded
1925	Member of TUC General Council	'Red Friday'
1926		General Strike
1928		Mond–Turner Talks Transport House opened
1929		Wall Street Crash Macmillan Committee on Finance
1931	Defeated as Labour candidate at Gateshead	
1936	President of TUC	
1938	Makes world tour	
1939		Second World War

	Career	*Events*
1940	Minister of Labour and National Service. MP for Central Wandsworth	Coalition Government formed
1941		Conscription of Women
1945	Foreign Secretary	Labour Government formed
1946		Treaty of Dunkirk
1947		Marshall Plan
1948		State of Israel created
		Treaty of Brussels
		Berlin Airlift
1949		North Atlantic Treaty
1950	MP for East Woolwich	Colombo Plan
1951	Lord Privy Seal Died – 14 April	Korean War

Bibliography

Bullock, Alan. *The Life and Times of Ernest Bevin.* William Heinemann Ltd, Vol. I, 1960; Vol. II, 1967.

Evans, Trevor. *Bevin.* George Allen & Unwin Ltd, 1946.

Williams, Francis. *Ernest Bevin.* Hutchinson & Co. Ltd, 1952.

Barclay, Sir Roderick. *Ernest Bevin and the Foreign Office.* Published by the author, 1975.

Tames, Richard. *Ernest Bevin.* Shire Publications Ltd, 1974.

Acheson, Dean. *Sketches from Life.* Hamish Hamilton Ltd, 1961.

Cole, G. D. H. *The Common People.* Methuen & Co. Ltd, 1938; 4th Edition, 1949.

Bevin, Ernest. *The Job to be Done.* William Heinemann Ltd, 1941.

Edwards, Huw T. *It was my Privilege.* Gee & Son Ltd, 1957.

Citrine, Lord. *Men and Work.* Hutchinson & Co. Ltd, 1964.

Citrine, Lord. *Two Careers.* Hutchinson & Co. Ltd, 1967.

Jenkins, Roy. *Nine Men of Power.* Hamish Hamilton Ltd, 1974.

MacDonald, D. F. *The State and the Trade Unions.* Macmillan Press Ltd, 1960; 2nd Edition, 1976.

Mortimer, Jim. *Ernest Bevin Memorial Lecture,* 1975.

Taylor, A. J. P. *Britain,* OUP, 1965.

Sked, Alan & Cook, Chris. *Post War Britain.* Penguin Books, 1979.

Symons, J. *The General Strike.* The Cresset Press, 1957.

Renshaw, Patrick. *The General Strike.* Eyre Methuen, 1975.

Farman, Christopher. *The General Strike May 1926.* Rupert Hart-Davis, 1972.

Pelling, Henry. *History of British Trade Unionism.* Penguin Books, 1976; 3rd Edition, 1976.

Churchill, W. S. *History of the Second World War.* Cassell Co. Ltd, 1948–54.

Wheeler Bennett, John. W. *King George VI.* Macmillan & Co. Ltd, 1958.

Bethell, Nicholas. *The Palestine Triangle*. Andre Deutsch Ltd, 1979.

Medlicott, W. N. *British Foreign Policy Since Versailles 1919–1963*. Methuen & Co. Ltd, 1940; 2nd Edition, 1968.

Macmillan, Harold. *Tides of Fortune*. Macmillan & Co. Ltd, 1969.

Strang, Lord. *Home and Abroad*. Andre Deutsch Ltd, 1956.

Nicolson, Harold, *Diaries & Letters 1954–1962*. Collins, 1968.

Johnston, G. A. *The International Labour Organization*. Europa Publications, 1970.

Young, G. M. *Stanley Baldwin*. Rupert Hart-Davis, 1952.

Ustinov, Peter. *Dear Me*. Penguin Books, 1977.

Lovell, John & Robert, B. C. *A Short History of the TUC*. Macmillan, 1968.

Golant, William. *Clem and Ernie. The Times*, 29 Nov. 1980.

Attlee, C. R. *As It Happened*. Heinemann, 1954.

Attlee, C. R. *A Portrait. The Observer*, 6 & 13 March 1960.

Williams, Francis. *Magnificent Journey*. The Rise of the Trade Unions. Odhams Press, 1954.

Index

141